the best **birdhouses** for your **backyard**

the best birdhouses
FOR YOUR backyard

MICHAEL BERGER

POPULAR WOODWORKING BOOKS

CINCINNATI, OHIO
www.popularwoodworking.com

READ THIS IMPORTANT SAFETY NOTICE

To prevent accidents, keep safety in mind while you work. Use the safety guards installed on power equipment; they are for your protection. When working on power equipment, keep fingers away from saw blades, wear safety goggles to prevent injuries from flying wood chips and sawdust, wear headphones to protect your hearing, and consider installing a dust vacuum to reduce the amount of airborne sawdust in your woodshop. Don't wear loose clothing, such as neckties or shirts with loose sleeves, or jewelry, such as rings, necklaces or bracelets, when working on power equipment. Tie back long hair to prevent it from getting caught in your equipment. People who are sensitive to certain chemicals should check the chemical content of any product before using it. The author and editors who compiled this book have tried to make the contents as accurate and correct as possible. Plans, illustrations, photographs and text have been carefully checked. All instructions, plans and projects should be carefully read, studied and understood before beginning construction. Due to the variability of local conditions, construction materials, skill levels, etc., neither the author nor Popular Woodworking Books assumes any responsibility for any accidents, injuries, damages or other losses incurred resulting from the material presented in this book.

METRIC CONVERSION CHART

to convert	to	multiply by
Inches	Centimeters	2.54
Centimeters	Inches	0.4
Feet	Centimeters	30.5
Centimeters	Feet	0.03
Yards	Meters	0.9
Meters	Yards	1.1
Sq. Inches	Sq. Centimeters	6.45
Sq. Centimeters	Sq. Inches	0.16
Sq. Feet	Sq. Meters	0.09
Sq. Meters	Sq. Feet	10.8
Sq. Yards	Sq. Meters	0.8
Sq. Meters	Sq. Yards	1.2
Pounds	Kilograms	0.45
Kilograms	Pounds	2.2
Ounces	Grams	28.4
Grams	Ounces	0.04

Visit our Web site at www.popularwoodworking.com for information and resources for woodworkers.

Other fine Popular Woodworking Books are available from your local bookstore or direct from the publisher.

05   04   03   02   01   5   4   3   2   1

Library of Congress Cataloging-in-Publication Data

Berger, Michael,
    The best birdhouses for your backyard / by Michael Berger.
        p. cm.
    Includes index.
    ISBN 1-55870-583-X (alk. paper)
    1. Birdhouses--Design and construction. I. Title.

QL676.5 .B39 2001
728'.927--dc21   2001018510

Edited by Jennifer Churchill
Designed by Brian Roeth
Interior art production by Kathy Gardner
Illustrations by Len Churchill
Cover and finished projects photographed by Al Parrish
Step photographs by Jennifer Churchill and Jim Stack
Production coordinated by Sara Dumford

dedication

To my mother, Marcella, who taught me what a rain crow was; to my father, Fred, for allowing me to lose more tools as a child than can be counted; and to my wife, Mary, for putting up with eccentricities and sawdust well past the point of reason, this book is lovingly dedicated.

about the author

Birds are nothing new to Michael Berger. Introduced as a small child to bird watching and bird feeding by his father and two great aunts, he has been actively finding ways to promote those activities in others ever since.

Over the years, he has received numerous commendations for his conservation efforts. As an Eagle Scout and assistant cubmaster for the Cub Scouts of America, Michael works at instilling his love for the outdoors in both children and adults alike. He is an avid caver and scuba diver, and is a member of the National Speleological Society.

acknowledgements

There are many people who deserve special mention with regard to the creation of this book. First, to Jim Stack and David Lewis for accepting my proposal, I owe my thanks. And to all the dedicated staff at Popular Woodworking Books: Jennifer Churchill, my talented editor; Brian Roeth, the designer, for creating such a wonderful package for this information; and to all the unsung heroes of the publishing world — the copyeditors, proofreaders, layout artists, indexers and production coordinators, many thanks.

There have been other special individuals throughout the years who have helped instill in me the knowledge and love of the outdoors. Stacy Doose, scout leader and caver extraordinaire, who got me hooked on caving and bats; George McElroy, who gave me my first birdhouse; and countless others with whom I have had the pleasure of hiking and birding over the years. Thank you for the wisdom and love of all things outdoors that you helped pass along.

table of contents

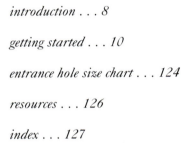

projects

introduction

One of my earliest memories is of birdhouses. I grew up out in the country, and spent the better part of my early years wandering around my one-acre yard, a yard with a fence that was made up of old-fashioned wooden posts and cross braces. About four feet up from the ground, birdhouses were attached to intermittent posts. My father had built them to attract bluebirds, wrens and other songbirds. And as I was a child, the birdhouses were one of the few things in our yard at my eye level. I would go from house to house, peeking in the holes to see who was home and if there

were any eggs. More than once I was rewarded with a flap of feathers in my face as the occupant beat wings for higher ground where it would be safe from the prying eyes of miniature humans.

As I grew older, one of my springtime duties was to patrol the fence line and repair any houses that had fallen on hard times. I'd drag an otherwise one-day chore out into a weekend endeavor, using every excuse I could think of to spend more time in tracking down nests, climbing trees and hauling out whatever tools I could get my hands on to effect those much-needed repairs. And after all these years, I still find just as much delight in providing shelter for our feathered neighbors as I did in my youth.

It is from this delight that this book

has sprung. The projects you'll find in these pages are not the fanciful, whimsical creations that speak of hours of coping-saw and decorative-painting work. Nor are they the creations of a master cabinetmaker, utilizing dovetails and other complex woodworking joinery and techniques. Those types of projects, though well-meaning and oftentimes beautiful to look at, don't always fill the genuine needs of birds.

The designs in this book are based on simple plans that have proven successful for me after years of trial-and-error construction and use. Most are so easy to construct that power tools aren't necessary — braces and handsaws can do the

job just fine. Some are more detailed, with complex miters and dadoes, but

none are so difficult that you wouldn't welcome some help from a young son or daughter. In fact, what better way to get your children interested in both woodworking and conservation — all at the same time?

The species covered in this book represent a broad range of birds generally found across the entire continent. The beauty of these designs is that many of them can be used just as successfully for other species of birds, as well. So feel free to adapt what you find here to fit the needs of your particular locale. And enjoy the fruits of your labor: the rewarding sight of a flash of color, a melodious song, and the knowledge that your efforts have helped preserve a piece of our natural heritage.

getting started

Birdhouses are not complex projects. Most are simple boxes, with perhaps a hinge here or miter there. You don't need a shop filled with expensive tools or years of woodworking experience to put a few birdhouses together. You don't need expensive lumber like quartersawn white oak, or fancy fixtures — just a few basic tools and a desire to put together a weather-tight home.

But there are a few special needs that these projects have, and questions you'll run into as you build these projects. For example, which woods hold up best against the elements? Are there types of wood that should be avoided? What types of hardware won't rust away into nothing? Which glues can survive the elements? The answers to these questions, and more, are all covered in this first chapter. I'll show you what has worked best for me over the years, and why. I'll explain my choice of tools, and give you hand-power options that will allow you to get the little ones involved in the building process. But most importantly, I'll show you how to have fun while providing shelter for our feathered friends at the same time.

Tools "for the Birds"

As I mentioned, building these birdhouses doesn't require a shop full of exotic and expensive power tools. In fact, you don't even need power at all — hand tools can do the job nicely.

circular saw blades

- *Pointed-tooth blade:*
  A multiple-toothed blade for crosscutting solid wood that leaves a reasonable finish.
- *Fine-tooth blade:*
  Used for fine, slow cuts in chipboard and plastic-laminated materials.
- *Rip blade:*
  A blade with large tungsten-carbide-tipped teeth; ideal for ripping softwoods. It also cuts hardwoods and man-made materials. Its cut tends to be rather rough.
- *Chisel-tooth blade:*
  A medium-priced universal saw blade suited to ripping and crosscutting softwoods, hardwoods and man-made material.
- *Carbide-tipped universal blade:*
  A top-quality universal blade that leaves an extremely fine finish when crosscutting or ripping solid woods and all man-made boards.

CIRCULAR SAWS — ONE WAY TO CUT
Though there are many different tools you can use to cut your lumber to size, one of my favorites is the circular saw. Mine is a Ryobi 13-amp model. It's great when I need to rip lumber, as I can attach the provided guide and get accurate rips every time.

TABLE SAWS AS TIME-SAVERS
Though you certainly don't need one of these tools to build great, functional birdhouses, a table saw can greatly speed up production, especially when you're tackling larger projects, such as a purple martin house.

Saws

Circular saws are the workhorses of birdhouse construction. They can rip and crosscut hardwoods, softwoods and man-made material with ease. They are light, portable and can accept a variety of blade types. A model that offers more features than you think you may need is a wise investment; the more you use this versatile tool, the more uses you'll find for it. Look for a model with an adjustable blade depth and a tilting blade — a must when cutting miters and dadoes. And remember to buy one that will handle the thickness of the material you'll be using. I've found the 7¼" models to be more than adequate. They can handle material up to 2⅜" thick, and will be more than you'll need for just about any birdhouse project.

If you happen to own one, a table saw can be a tremendous time-saver, especially when you decide to tackle a larger project, such as a purple-martin house where there are numerous rips and crosscuts involved. Though not essential to building — in fact, you can achieve great results without one — a table saw can also add to overall accuracy. You don't even need an expensive model to do the trick. I've used a benchtop model that was far from a professional grade; I would never trust it if furniture construction was involved. But it was light, inexpensive and portable.

Jigsaws are great for handling curves, or for cutting lumber down into more manageable sizes. I use a Skil 4445 4-amp orbital action model. Orbital action can be a great time saver when cutting lumber with a jigsaw. When the orbital action is engaged, the blade moves slightly forward on the upstroke and slightly back on the downstroke, thus removing more material per cut. The downside to this is that the cut can be a bit ragged. The nice thing about the Skil 4445 is that the orbital action is adjustable, and can be turned off completely for a more finished cut.

Jigsaw Blades

LENGTH	TOOTH SIZE/PITCH	SET	USE
3"	8tpi/3mm	Side set	Hardwood and softwood, up to 2¼" thick. Especially good for rip and rough cutting.
3"	6tpi/4mm	Ground & side set	As above, but with a cleaner cut.
3"	6tpi/4mm	Ground	Hardwood, softwood and man-made boards up to 2½" thick; very clean cut.
2"	12tpi/2mm	Wavy set	Man-made boards up to 1¼" thick; very fine cut.
2"	12tpi/2mm	Wavy set	For cutting tight curves in wood up to ¾" thick.
3"	10tpi/2.5mm	Ground	Reversed teeth to cut on the downstroke; usually used for plastic-laminated boards.

JIGSAWS — ANOTHER WAY TO CUT

A close second in cutting tools is the versatile saber saw (or jigsaw). I usually use a Skil 4-amp variable-speed orbital action model. Orbital action is a great benefit on saber saws, as it enables you to control the finesse of the cut — either remove large amounts of material per cut for faster action, or dial it down and remove small bits at a time for smoother cuts.

cordless circular saws?

Over the past few years, battery technology has reached a point where it can finally handle the power draw of a tool such as a circular saw. Cordless saws are now lighter, more powerful and more convenient than ever before. And even though the blades tend to be smaller than on the corded models, they'll handle just about any birdhouse need with ease. Just remember to keep a spare charged battery handy — these tools still eat battery life at an amazing rate.

tip

MOTOR SIZE

Nearly all electric jigsaws have 350W motors capable of top speeds of about 3,000 strokes per minute. Don't be fooled when you see a motor rated higher than this — it's designed to handle thicker material, not necessarily cut any faster.

Power Drills and Rotary Tools

Cordless tools have revolution-ized woodworking and home improve-ment. If you've ever had to deal with a tangled ex-tension cord, you'll quickly agree that cordless tools, especially drills, are a godsend. I use a Craftsman 15.6-volt model. Though it's an oddball in power rating (I've never seen another 15.6-volt model), it does the job admirably, and when bought as a set with a case, charger and extra battery, it is quite reasonably priced. Another benefit of a cordless drill is that you can take it with you to the yard as you install your bird-houses, without having to string togeth-er multiple extension cords.

My Dremel variable-speed MotoTool comes in handy for all sorts of uses — from sanding the insides of openings to etching to easing corners and edges (when combined with Dremel's router attachment).

Sanders

Sanding is always the crowning glory of any woodworking project, and for years I've used nothing but orbital palm sanders. But when it came to birdhous-es, I needed something different — more like a detail sander but with the ability to sand an entire piece. I found my solution in the Black & Decker Mouse. The point on the Mouse makes it a piece of cake to get into tight corners, and I've found it to be a great little sander for all my birdhouse projects. The sanding sheets attach with hook-and-loop fasteners, and the tips are re-placeable apart from the main sheet.

Other Tools

As I mentioned earlier, you don't need a dedicated woodshop to make birdhous-es. In fact, when I was building the proj-ects for this book (and living in Key West at the time, where space is at a premium), I was forced to work out on my back deck. For those of you also forced to work in small spaces, like in a corner of a garage, thank the stars that

CORDLESS DRILLS
A must-have for any woodworker or handy-man, a cordless drill makes life easy and tangle-free. My model is a Craftsman 15.6V variable-speed model. There are many great brands on the market — just make sure you buy one that suits the type of work you intend to use it for.

THE ROTARY CLUB
I'm a huge fan of rotary tools, and have more attachments for mine than I can shake a stick at. They come in handy for easing corners, carving and routing, sanding — you name it, a rotary tool can proba-bly do it. I use a Dremel variable-speed MotoTool.

SANDING
Though sanding isn't nearly as necessary when building birdhouses as it is when doing other woodworking projects, I still enjoy putting a nice surface on my projects. Shown here is a random orbital sander, which works great for sanding these projects. I've also found the Black & Decker Mouse sander to be a handy, general-purpose sander for almost any birdhouse project.

someone invented the Workmate. This handy little device is part workbench and part vise, all rolled into one unit that folds up for easy storage. There are a few different models now on the market, but all of them include provisions for dual-height work surfaces, clamping and pinning. Some of the more expensive models can even be cranked down with only one hand. And because of their durability (I've had mine for over 15 years now), they are worth every penny.

Miscellaneous Hand Tools

Many of the tools needed to build birdhouses are probably things you already have lying around the house. A good-quality hammer, sets of chisels (they don't have to be fancy or expensive for our needs here), and some form of measuring device are all necessary.

A HELPING HAND
Black & Decker's Workmate can get you out of many a tight fix, with its ability to clamp and pin just about anything.

OTHER HAND TOOLS
Some other tools you'll want to have around are a good, sturdy hammer; a folding rule (or measuring tape); chisels in a variety of sizes; and a bevel gauge (handy when transposing angles for roof lines).

a case for cases

Many of my woodworking friends scoff at my infatuation with a well-made tool case. But just because you think the tool will spend more time out of the case than in it, don't discount the value of a good case. If you don't have a dedicated woodshop, cases can make it easier to stack and store your tools, and they certainly help to keep dust and debris out of the motors. And for those of you with young, curious hands prowling around the house, a case prevents them from handling sharp blades.

TAPE MEASURES

When purchasing a tape measure, make sure to choose one with a strong, stiff blade that won't bend or kink. Also, consider getting one longer than you think you might need — that way, if an oddball measuring situation comes along, you won't find yourself shortchanged.

COMBINATION SQUARE

One of my favorite tools for birdhouse construction is the combination square. You can preset the length by loosening the thumb nut, and the fixed 90° and 45° angles are invaluable in construction.

Tape Measures and Clamps

When it comes to measuring, you have a wide variety of choices. One of my favorites is the tried-and-true folding rule. It's been around for over 100 years, and for the dimensions we'll be dealing with in these projects, it's ideal. Tape measures, metal rules and combination squares are other options for measuring.

And while we're talking about measuring, don't overlook the useful bevel gauge. Used for marking and laying out angles, a bevel gauge can be an invaluable aid to your work. You can set specified angles by holding it up against a protractor, and then transferring that angle to either your workpiece or to the blade of your table saw.

After your parts are measured and cut, you'll need to clamp them together. The aforementioned Workmate can help in this department, but you'll really need some

EXTRA HANDS

Clamps can act as an extra set of hands to hold parts together, or provide pressure while glue sets up. I've found the most handy to be these Quick-Grip clamps. They come in a variety of sizes for every need, and the rubber pads keep the ends from marring the surfaces being clamped.

HOLE SAWS

For cutting the entrance holes for birdhouses, get yourself a hole saw set with diameters running from 1" to 3½".

BRACE YOURSELF

Who said power was absolutely necessary? This Stanley traditional brace will do the job of drilling entrance holes just as admirably as a cordless drill.

A DRILL FOR ASSEMBLY

This Miller Falls No. 5A hand drill is a useful tool for drilling smaller assembly and drainage holes. It's also handy when you want to involve young hands in the building process.

the wood at a steady pace.

But what if you prefer to work without power tools? Regular hand tools, whose designs have remained unchanged for years, will do the job just fine. The traditional brace excels at drilling holes, especially the larger entrance holes (when used in conjunction with expansion bits). For smaller assemblies or drainage holes, I sometimes use a hand drill (also known as a wheel brace). These types of tools not only provide me a sense of history and a feeling of personal satisfaction, but also allow me to involve young children in the building process, as there is less chance of injury when you take power out of the equation.

Glues

I use only two types of glue in my birdhouse projects: waterproof carpenter's glue and polyurethane glue. Carpenter's glue, such as Elmer's brand, has been around for years, is easy to work with and easy to clean up. Polyurethane glue is a fairly recent development, and I've grown quite fond of it for birdhouse construction. I've even built entire houses using nothing but polyurethane glue to hold them together, and they're still going strong. Polyurethane glues also have gap-filling properties, especially useful when you're dealing with irregular or rough-cut wood.

Choosing Hardware

Just as there are special considerations when purchasing lumber, the same holds true for hardware. Though almost any kind of fastener can be used to put a birdhouse together, only certain types will provide reliable service during years of hard-weather exposure. The last thing you want to see is your beautifully constructed birdhouse falling apart because your hardware wasn't up to the challenges of Mother Nature. Luckily we have some options.

For example, one choice is galva-

dedicated clamps to complete the job right. There are many different types of clamps on the market, but my favorite for this type of work is the Quick-Grip clamp. It holds strong and fast, comes in many different sizes to meet just about any need, and can be easily adjusted or released with just a squeeze. And though easily adjusted or released with just a squeeze. And though these types of clamps can run anywhere from $12 to $25 apiece, invest the money and buy a few more than you think you'll need. It never fails that once

you're into a critical stage of construction, you realize too late that you're one clamp short to do the job right.

Hole Saws and Hand Drills

A hole saw is a cylindrical-shaped saw blade held in a backing plate that is mounted to a twist drill running through the center. Hole saws are sold in sets ranging from 1" to 3½" in diameter. When you use a hole saw, drill more slowly than you would usually (as the blade will spin much faster than the center drill), and feed the blade into

TYPICAL HARDWARE

Though your choices are wide when it comes to hardware, I've found these items to be especially well-suited to birdhouse construction. Shown here, from left to right, are a ringshank stainless-steel nail, a galvanized finishing nail, a drywall screw and an audiovisual cable bracket which I use as a pivoting lock for swinging inspection panels.

EXPANSION BITS AND COUNTERSINKS

When used in conjunction with a brace, these expansion bits will do the job of cutting entrance holes quite nicely. With the three shown here you can cut holes anywhere from 1" to over 4" in diameter. The bit on the far left is a countersink, handy when you want to make sure the heads of your assembly screws sit flush with the surface.

WING DIVIDERS

This tool is especially handy if you need to transfer a specific measurement from one project to another. Simply set the points of the divider to the measurement you're duplicating, and then transfer the divider to the workpiece.

STICKY STUFF

I use two types of glue for my projects — a waterproof carpenter's wood glue (in this case, Elmer's) and polyurethane glue (both Probond and Gorilla Glue brands). The polyurethane glue is particularly useful when you need a waterproof, gap-filling adhesive.

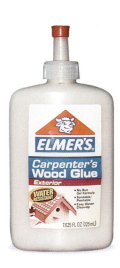

A THIRD HAND FOR DRIVING SCREWS

This driver bit from DeWalt is a real headache-preventer. It mounts in your drill just like a regular screwdriver bit, and is magnetized like a regular bit. But this driver has a sliding sleeve that slips down over the screw head and body, leaving just the tip of the screw exposed, thus effectively holding it in place while you drive it home.

nized weather-resistant hardware. In the galvanizing process, the hardware is tumbled in molten zinc to form a weather-resistant coating. There are variations of this process, such as electrogalvanizing, that also coats the hardware with zinc, but these other processes leave a thinner zinc coating and produce a less weather-resistant product.

Another option, and one of my favorites despite the higher cost, is stainless-steel hardware. Usually sold by the pound, you can purchase just the

amount you need and no more. Though stainless steel is quite a bit higher in price than galvanized hardware, I'd recommend it for any project in which you've used a more expensive wood, such as redwood or cypress, or on projects that you expect to last for years.

Nails

Nails are traditionally sold in sizes called "penny sizes." The sizes start with a twopenny (2d) nail that is 1" in length. A fourpenny (4d) nail is 1½" long; a sixpenny (6d) nail is 2" long,

tip

If you'll be using screws for your birdhouse construction and you're also using finished lumber, consider drywall screws as an economical alternative to galvanized hardware.

appearance grading in plywood

Plywood is commonly graded by appearance. A typical system uses the letters A, B, C and D. The A grade is the best quality, being smooth-cut with virtually no defects. The D grade is the poorest, having the maximum amount of permitted defects, such as knots, splits and discolorations. Each sheet will also be graded for each side individually. For example, an A-A grade sheet would have two faces that are of exceptional quality, while a B-C grade sheet would have one face of B grade and one of C grade. When buying sheets of different grades per face, always place the best face out in your construction, and leave the rougher side facing inward where young birds can take advantage of it as a climbing aid when it's time to leave the nest box.

and so forth.

I use nails a lot building my birdhouses — you just can't beat them for their versatility. When buying nails for your projects, make sure you purchase nails that are twice as long as the thickness of the material you are nailing together. For example, if you're using 1" true-thickness material, then purchase nails that are 2" in length.

Screws

Like nails, screws have their own language. For example, screws are sold by a number that designates the diameter — the larger the number, the thicker the screw (for example, a No. 8 screw would be thicker than a No. 6 screw). Screws are also sold by length. To get the size that's right for your project, just combine the thickness number with

tip

If you live in a cold climate, consider using ringshank nails, which have a series of ribs running down the length of the nail shaft. This type of nail is far less likely to pull out due to the swelling and shrinking of the wood that the freezing process causes.

the length (as in No. 6 × 2").

When purchasing screws for your projects, stay away from standard-head screws. Phillips-head screws provide better grip for your screwdriver, and are less likely to tear out during the installation process.

Choosing Your Lumber

The nice thing about birdhouses is that you can use almost any kind of lumber, and don't have to spend God's own fortune on materials. I've used everything from pine to plywood to salvaged barn siding. Birds aren't picky and, frankly, some of the most effective birdhouses I've seen have been made out of the oldest, knottiest, most decrepit wood imaginable.

Unless you have access to a jointer and planer, you'll want to purchase dimensional lumber rather than rough lumber. Finished lumber has already been planed and smoothed and is ready to cut to size. When selecting boards, look for any obvious defects, such as warping or cupping, and avoid these pieces. And remember that finished lumber is always slightly smaller than its given size (see "Given vs. Actual Lumber Sizes" chart for the size differences).

Cypress

Also known as bald cypress, southern cypress, red cypress or yellow cypress, this wood comes from the southern and south Atlantic states, and is not as available as it was several decades ago. Other variations of this softwood are native to the Mediterranean, parts of Africa, areas of the California coast and throughout the Caribbean. I got hooked on cypress when I lived in Key West, Florida, and it quickly became one of my personal favorites. It was commonly used in house construction down in the Keys and throughout the Caribbean islands back in the late 1800s, and many of those homes are still standing today. Wonderfully rot- and insect-resistant, it weathers to a beautiful silver-gray and provides decades of service. Cypress can be difficult to find in many parts of the country, but can always be special-

Given vs. Approximate Lumber Sizes

GIVEN SIZE	APPROXIMATE SIZE
1×4	$3/4" \times 3 1/2"$
1×6	$3/4" \times 5 1/2"$
1×8	$3/4" \times 7 1/2"$
1×10	$3/4" \times 9 1/4"$
1×12	$3/4" \times 11 1/4"$
2×4	$1 1/2" \times 3 1/2"$
4×4	$3 1/2" \times 3 1/2"$

ordered. One thing to remember when working with cypress is that it can be difficult to nail, so remember to predrill all holes and you'll be fine.

Western Red Cedar

This wood is another great choice for building birdhouses, and is certainly easier to find than cypress. Weather-resistant, rot-resistant, insect-resistant — western red cedar has it all. It is light, strong and, over time, weathers to a beautiful silver-gray just as cypress does. Cedar often comes with one side rough and one smooth. Use this feature to your advantage and place the rough surfaces facing the interior of the birdhouse. That way, the nestlings will have something to grab hold of as they work their way up towards the entrance hole when they're ready to fledge. The major drawback to cedar is that it splits very easily, and everything must be predrilled. Cedar is also very expensive, but the cost will pay for itself over time since the wood is so long-lasting.

pressure-treated lumber

Except as a mounting post, under no circumstances use any type of treated lumber in your birdhouse construction projects. Pressure-treated lumber stands out from other woods as it has a slightly greenish tint. This color comes from chromated copper-arsenate, a deadly poison. Personally, I even stay away from this material as a mounting post, and prefer to use cedar posts whenever possible.

Douglas Fir

Another of my personal favorites, Douglas fir (also known as British Columbia pine or Oregon pine) is also quite weather- and rot-resistant, and is less expensive than cedar or cypress. It's as easy to work as pine, and the grain can be quite interesting and appealing to the eye (earlywood and latewood grain patterns are different, and can be very attractive). The major drawback to Douglas fir is its availability — you may have to special order it as it's not as readily found in all parts of the country.

Redwood

Another rot-resistant wood, redwood isn't the best choice for birdhouses for two main reasons. First, redwood is very susceptible to splitting and cracking. Second, it is very expensive. Redwood does come in handy for mounting posts, but I've found it to be simply too finicky and expensive for my tastes.

Pine

Birdhouses are the perfect project for inexpensive pine. Light, easy to work, and inexpensive, it's the wood of choice when I'm building a lot of birdhouses at one time. Though not as weather- and rot-resistant as cedar, fir or cypress, it can still deliver 10 years or better of service before giving out — I've had some birdhouses built from pine last for over 15 years. The biggest drawback to pine is that it tends to warp over time, so choose the best boards you can at the time of purchase. And place your pine-built projects in a more sheltered location, such as up against your house or in a thicket of trees.

Plywood

The jury is out on the use of exterior plywood in birdhouse projects. I've used it many times, especially when building purple martin houses, but some experts don't agree with this application. Plywood is manufactured using formaldehyde, a carcinogen that is harmful to wildlife as well as people. The real question is how much off-gassing of formaldehyde occurs over time and if it dissipates at a greater rate when it is always outdoors in the elements. Generally, I recommend steering away from plywood except for use in purple martin houses. Plywood can greatly reduce the weight of the house, and your back will be happy with that when you go to raise the house. If you do use plywood, make sure to purchase only exterior-grade or marine-grade plywood — otherwise you'll run into problems of the plywood delaminating due to exposure to moisture.

Hardwoods

For a change of pace, why not try building a birdhouse out of scrap hardwood you have lying around the shop? I've used oak and poplar many times over the years, as the scraps have allowed, and have had wonderful results.

shop wisdom

- Make sure you have a push stick or push block within easy reach before starting a cut or machining operation. Don't get into awkward positions in which a sudden slip could make your hand hit the blade or cutter.
- Double-check your wood for loose knots, nails and other hazards. If not noticed, these can cause injury and damage your equipment.
- Always wear goggles, safety glasses, or a face mask when using cutting tools. When sanding, wear a dust mask as well. If you're using an extremely loud tool, wear hearing protection. Never wear neckties, work gloves, bracelets, wristwatches, or loose clothing. For long hair, wear a cap or tie it back.
- Be sure your guards and antikickback devices are in good working order and in their correct positions. Before using a blade or cutter, check to make sure it is sharp and clean.
- Make sure the floor surface in your workshop is dry, hard-wearing, nontrip and nonslip (no steps, level changes, slopes), fireproof and easy to clean. Most workshops have a solid concrete slab. For additional traction (for instance, in front of a lathe), a low-cost solution is to paint a selected area of the floor with rubber-type adhesive, sprinkle sand on it, and sweep away the remaining sand after the adhesive has dried. Additionally, rubber mats serve as portable nonslip and antifatigue floor surfaces.
- Some specific tasks (or left- and right-handedness) can require additional or adjustable lighting. You may want to install lamps as side lights where more light is needed. Portable light stands are also helpful.
- Provide visitors, especially children, with safety goggles and make sure everyone stays a safe distance away from equipment. Keep in mind that many machines (for instance, portable planers) spit out waste at a child's eye level. If you have a workshop at home with children, educate them in the safe use of the machines. When not in the workshop, remove start-up keys and lock the workshop. You may want to consider padlocking the machines.
- Every workshop needs fire detection and prevention equipment. Install smoke or fire detectors, and keep at least one class ABC fire extinguisher in an easy-access location. Never throw water onto machinery that is still plugged in.

american robin
nesting shelf

To many folks, the American robin is the first bird of spring. Though many of these friendly birds would winter in our woods in southern Ohio, as a child I would always keep a sharp eye out for the first one I could spot after the snows melted. And even after I learned that other species, such as the red-winged blackbird, arrived earlier than the migrating robins, it has remained etched in my mind that the sight of a robin is a sure sign that spring is just around the corner.

This simple nesting shelf is easy to construct, and is a great first project for novices. There are only five parts to this shelf, and all the cuts are very straightforward. I built the example here out of cypress — an extremely rot-resistant wood — because I was after a look that was different from pine or cedar (though just about any wood will work fine).

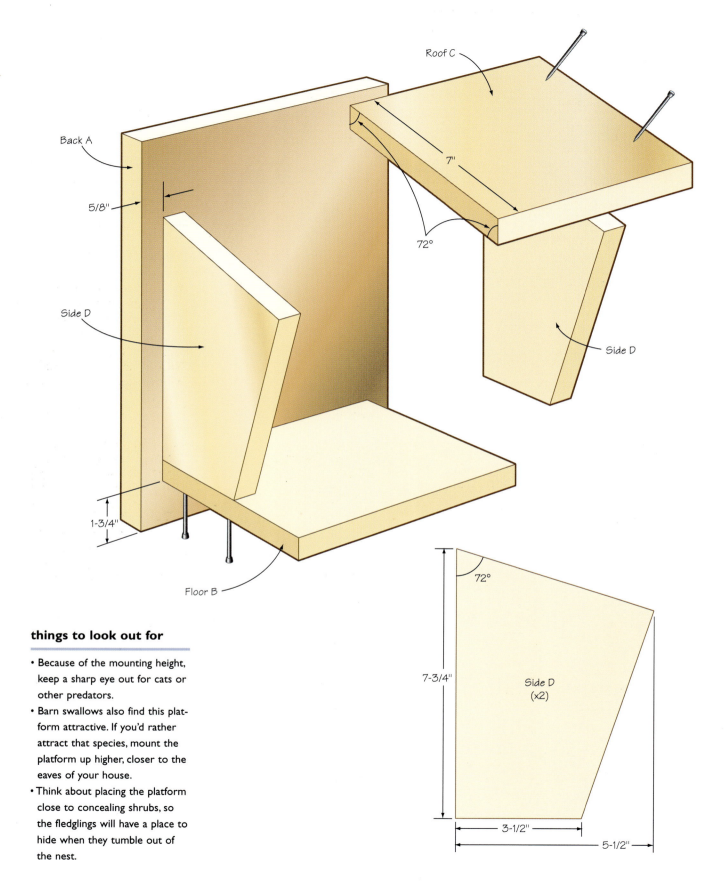

Roof C

Back A

5/8"

Side D

72°

7"

Side D

1-3/4"

Floor B

72°

7-3/4"

Side D
(x2)

3-1/2"

5-1/2"

things to look out for

- Because of the mounting height, keep a sharp eye out for cats or other predators.
- Barn swallows also find this platform attractive. If you'd rather attract that species, mount the platform up higher, closer to the eaves of your house.
- Think about placing the platform close to concealing shrubs, so the fledglings will have a place to hide when they tumble out of the nest.

american robin nesting shelf

Schedule of Materials: **AMERICAN ROBIN NESTING SHELF**

LETTER	QUANTITY	PART	STOCK	THICKNESS	WIDTH	LENGTH	COMMENTS
A	1	Back	1×10	³/₄	9¹/₄	12⁷/₈	
B	1	Floor	1×10	³/₄	7	8	
C	1	Roof	1×10	³/₄	8¹/₄	8	
D	2	Sides	1×10	³/₄	7³/₄	5¹/₂	

Hardware and Supplies

• 1¹/₂" galvanized finishing nails or 1⁵/₈" galvanized screws

• Waterproof glue

About the American Robin

As familiar as baseball and apple pie, the American robin is probably the most recognized bird in North America. It was originally named by British colonists because of its similarity to the robin of England (a small, hedgerow bird with a red breast).

The American robin, a true thrush, is one of the largest and most numerous of American thrushes.

The male is olive-gray; the top and sides of the head are black; the chin and throat are white with black streaks, and the breast and underparts are reddish orange.

The female has duller hues. Juveniles are dark on top, much like the adult's plumage, but the feathers of the back, upper wings and rump have streaks of white and blackish tips, giving the upperparts a speckled appearance. The cinnamon coloring of the breast is overlaid with conspicuous black spots. There is much individual variation in the cinnamon color of the underparts; some juveniles are largely white underneath. This plumage molts sometime between August and October, depending on when the individual hatched.

The American robin migrates and lives close to human dwellings. Each spring, robins will usually migrate back to the same area year after year. Males stake out their territories before the females arrive, and then sing love songs to the females. From early fall until spring, the males do not sing, but chatter and call. Females call, but leave the singing to the males.

vital statistics

American Robin

(Turdus migratorius)

SIZE:
9" to 11"

NUMBER OF EGGS:
3 to 5

LENGTH OF INCUBATION:
Approximately 12 days

BROODS PER SEASON:
2 to 3

FOOD:
Insects, worms, grubs, snails and other invertebrates, fruit, berries

RANGE:
Summer, across the United States, as far north as Alaska; winter, south to Mexico

1 | **CUT TO SIZE**

Cut the back, floor and roof to size as indicated in the Schedule of Materials. Remember that the roof will need to have its back edge cut at an 18° angle to match the slope of the sides.

House Placement

Robins are not choosy nesters. They will build practically anywhere. But for placement of this nesting platform, there are a few things to keep in mind. Try to choose a site that's not too close to a door or traffic area — constant comings and goings will likely scare the mother off her eggs. I've had great luck placing the platform near a window so I could watch the developing brood.

Don't place the platform too high off the ground. Though you may run a higher risk of predation, it's important not to have the nest so high that fledglings could get hurt as they flutter to the ground. Baby robins can't really fly when they leave the nest. They sort of make a controlled crash to the ground and just walk about and hide in underbrush for a few days until they are able to take to the skies. So don't be tempted to try to catch a baby robin and place it back in the nest. The father will be close by, and will continue to feed and care for the young as they mature.

2 | **SHAPE THE SIDES**

Cut the sides according to the Schedule of Materials. The easiest way to do this is to first cut out the sides as $7^{3}/_{4}$" $\times$ $5^{1}/_{2}$" rectangles. Then mark an 18° slope for the roof and cut the top to the correct angle. Finally, from the front point of the top of the side, draw a line down to a point $3^{1}/_{2}$" out from the bottom back corner, and make your cut along that line. Remember to make two sides.

3 | **DRILL PILOT HOLES**

Draw a line across the back piece 2" up from the bottom edge (this line marks where you'll attach the floor). Then drill three equally spaced pilot holes $^{3}/_{8}$" up from that line through the back.

4 | **ATTACH THE FLOOR**

Using $1^{5}/_{8}$" galvanized screws or $1^{1}/_{2}$" galvanized finishing nails and either waterproof carpenter's glue or polyurethane glue, attach the floor to the back at the line you previously drew.

5 | **ATTACH THE SIDES**

Then attach the sides to the floor and back.

6 | **ADD THE ROOF**

Finally, attach the roof to the sides and the back. Then with sandpaper or a sander, smooth out all surfaces and lightly round over all the edges.

to paint, or not to paint?

When it comes to birdhouse finishes, I'm a purist. If I can help it, I don't use any finish at all. The way I look at it, birds are more attracted to houses that look natural. And since the bark of trees (which would cover their natural homes) usually isn't found in bright, vibrant colors, I try to stick to an appearance that's as close to the look of a tree as I can. Also, birds generally don't want their nests to stand out and attract attention. Bright colors advertise "Come and look over here!" Besides, many finishes can be toxic, and the last thing you want to do is poison the very bird you're trying to attract.

Some of the birdhouses you see in this book were painted merely to increase their visibility in the photographs. The only birdhouses I routinely paint are purple martin houses and bat houses, but I'll go into that with each of these individual projects. As a rule, stay as natural as possible. If you feel really compelled to paint your project, pick colors that are soft and not too bright — country pastels are good choices. Use only a waterproof nontoxic latex paint, and never apply any of the finish to either the interior of the box or to the inside edges of the entrance holes. If you must use paint, use it sparingly, and not where it will come into contact with the resident of the house.

house wren
nesting box

When I was six or seven years old, a co-worker of my father by the name of George McElroy gave me my very first birdhouse. It was a small Crisco can covered in bark, with a conical roof and an eye-hook at the point for hanging. I'm not sure if the little house was meant for wrens, but it sure did the trick. I spent many an hour at our picnic table secretly spying on the comings and goings of this comical little bird. Watching it flit from perch to perch as it sang its merry little song brightened up even the dreariest day. And I am forever grateful to George, whom I referred to ever after as the "birdhouse man," for getting me hooked on birdhouses.

This box is quite easy to construct, and is a natural progression for young hands after tackling the robin nesting platform. I built the example here from pine, as I was planning to mount this box where I felt the elements would really take a toll on it. But just about any weather-resistant wood will work.

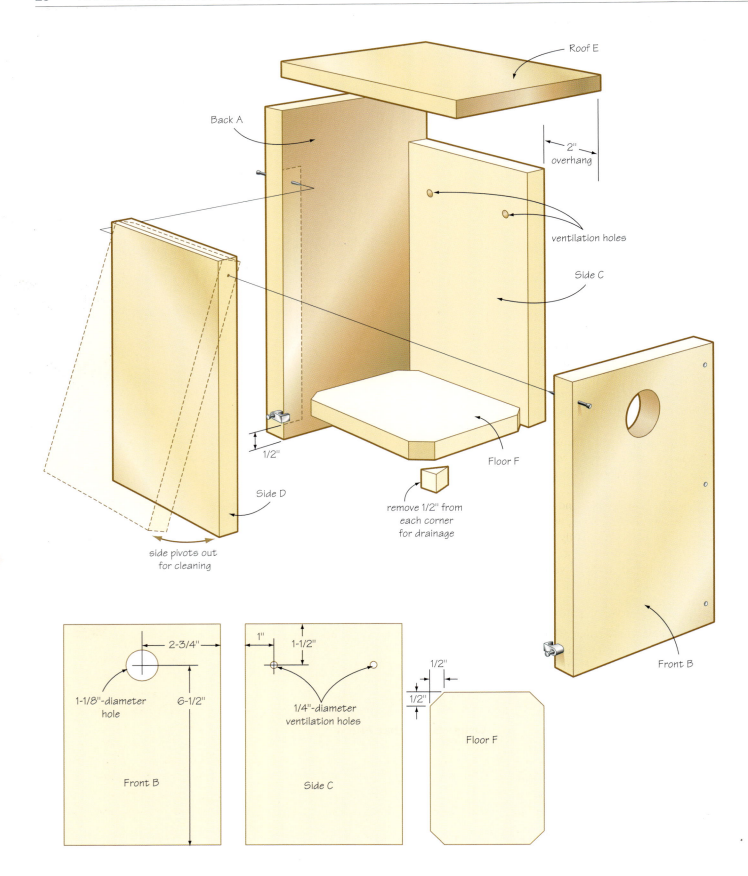

Roof E

Back A

2"
overhang

ventilation holes

Side C

1/2"

Side D

Floor F

remove 1/2" from
each corner
for drainage

side pivots out
for cleaning

Front B

2-3/4"

1-1/8"-diameter
hole

6-1/2"

Front B

1"

1-1/2"

1/4"-diameter
ventilation holes

Side C

1/2"

1/2"

Floor F

house wren nesting box

Schedule of Materials: **HOUSE WREN NESTING BOX**

LETTER	QUANTITY	PART	STOCK	THICKNESS	WIDTH	LENGTH	COMMENTS
A	I	Back	I×6	$3/4$	$5^{1}/_{2}$	II	
B	I	Front	I×6	$3/4$	$5^{1}/_{2}$	8	Center a $1^{1}/_{8}$" hole $6^{1}/_{2}$" from bottom.
C	I	Side	I×6	$3/4$	$5^{1}/_{2}$	8	Drill two $1/4$" ventilation holes.
D	I	Side	I×6	$3/4$	$5^{1}/_{2}$	$7^{3}/_{4}$	This side shorter to allow hinging.
E	I	Roof	I×6	$3/4$	$5^{1}/_{2}$	$8^{1}/_{4}$	
F	I	Floor	I×6	$3/4$	4	$5^{1}/_{2}$	

Hardware and Supplies

• $1^{1}/_{2}$" galvanized finishing nails or $1^{5}/_{8}$" galvanized screws

• Audiovisual cable stays (to serve as locks on the pivoting side)

• Waterproof glue

About the House Wren

House wrens, and indeed all wren species, are very social, energetic birds. Their light, burbling song, combined with their trick of flicking their tail up and down while perched, is a sight that you'll not soon forget. These little birds just look as if they are always having the time of their lives!

Besides the house wren, there are two other common wren types — the Carolina wren and Bewick's wren. The ranges of all three species overlap somewhat.

The Carolina wren is found most often east of the Mississippi, while Bewick's wren is found primarily throughout the South and Southwest. And since the house wren also covers those same areas, pay close attention to your nest builder to see which you've managed to attract.

Bewick's wren has a long white eyebrow, and the Carolina wren has a distinctive white throat patch in addition to the white eyebrow. As the house wren has neither, it shouldn't be too difficult to tell them apart.

Wrens are not all that picky in their nesting site choices. I've found them nesting in old boots, on top of stumps, in watering cans and, of course, in nesting boxes. Wrens will also attempt to build several nests in various sites, and will not hesitate to chase off intruders, be they other birds or humans, as they construct their homes. I've lost count of the times I've been driven away by an industrious, yet extremely territorial wren that was engrossed in nest building.

House Placement

With wrens being so accommodating, house placement is a little less critical than with other species. Semi-open habitats are best, with trees or shrubs nearby. I've had great luck with house placement along old fencerows, where the house is bolted to the top of the wooden post. Wrens are also one of the few species that will use hanging houses. I'm especially fond of this option in areas where snakes or stray cats pose a danger to either eggs or nestlings. I've also found that wrens prefer sunny rather than shady locations, so if you do mount the box in or near trees, make sure the spot you choose, which should be anywhere from 4 to 8 feet off the ground, gets a good deal of sunlight throughout the day.

Other Birds that Might Use This Box

• Carolina wren
• Bewick's wren
• Black-capped chickadee
• Carolina chickadee

vital statistics

House Wren

(*Troglodytes aedon*)

SIZE:
$4^{1}/_{2}$" to $5^{1}/_{4}$" long

NUMBER OF EGGS:
5 to 8

LENGTH OF INCUBATION:
12 to 15 days

BROODS PER SEASON:
2 or 3

FOOD:
Insects, spiders and snails

RANGE:
Summer, continental United States to southern Canada; winter, southern states to Mexico

tip

Raccoons are terrible predators of bird nests. If you have problems with raccoons in your area, consider securing the inspection side of the birdhouse with a screw through the front instead of using the audiovisual cable stays. That way, unless they learn how to use screwdrivers, the raccoons' efforts will be thwarted every time!

things to look out for

Make sure the entrance hole is small enough to prohibit sparrows from using the nest box.

Swallows and bluebirds may also be attracted to these boxes, so make sure to build enough for each species you're attempting to attract.

Keep a close eye out for stray cats on the prowl, as they are the wren's No. 1 enemy.

Field mice also seem to be fond of this house design, so make sure the nest builder is of the feathered variety, not the four-footed type.

1

MEASURE

Measure out the parts according to the dimensions in the Schedule of Materials. As you mark everything out, remember to allow for the material that the saw will remove with each cut (commonly known as the "kerf"). And remember to mark one side piece $1/4$" shorter than the other, as that side will serve as the cleaning and inspection door.

2

CUT TO SIZE

With a circular saw, jigsaw or table saw, cut the pieces to size based on the measurements you just made. Always wear safety glasses when working with power tools, and keep fingers well clear of the spinning blades.

3

ALLOW FOR VENTILATION

Drill two $1/4$" air holes $1 1/2$" down from the top in each of the two sides.

house wren nesting box

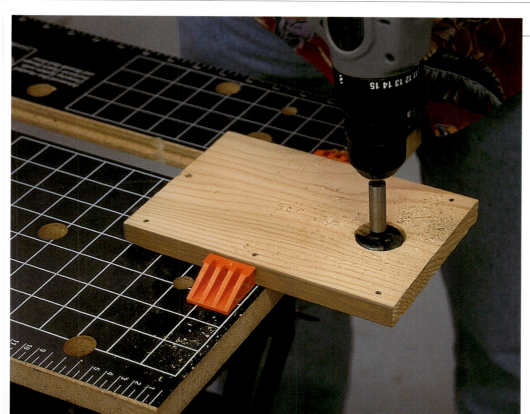

4

DRILL THE ENTRANCE

With your hole saw, drill a 1⅛" entrance hole in the front piece. Center the hole 6½" up from the bottom edge of the front piece. Remember to let the drill work slowly, as it can overheat if you try to force it to work faster by pushing down harder. And if you're using a cordless drill and building multiple birdhouses, have a spare battery on hand and recharge often, as drilling entrance holes can chew through your battery fairly quickly. If you don't have a hole saw, a Forstner bit will also do the job of cutting the opening, as shown here.

5

ORGANIZE THE PARTS

Once you have everything cut to size, you should have parts that look like this.

6

ADD ONE SIDE

After drilling three pilot holes, attach the right side (as you're looking at the front of the birdhouse) to the back with waterproof glue and $1^5/_8$" galvanized screws or $1^1/_2$" finishing nails.

7

ATTACH THE FRONT

Then, in the same way, attach the front to the side.

8

ATTACH THE BOTTOM

Cut off $1/_2$" from each of the corners of the bottom (these holes will allow drainage). Then attach the bottom to the back, side and front assembly. Remember to position the floor so that it is flush with the sides and front.

house wren nesting box

9

In the same manner as you attached the other pieces, secure the roof to the birdhouse.

10 **ADD THE LEFT SIDE**

Now attach the left (inspection) side. To allow for the hinging movement, first align the side so that its bottom edge is flush with the floor. Clamp the unit together, and near the top, drill two pilot holes (one through the front and one through the back) into the side. Then drive home a 1½" galvanized finishing nail in each of the pilot holes to serve as pivot points.

11 **SECURE THE INSPECTION SIDE**

Nail two audiovisual cable stays into the edges of both the front and back to serve as rotating locks to keep the inspection side closed. If you have problems with raccoons getting into nesting boxes, you can also use screws to lock the inspection side in place. Then sand everything down, and you're all set!

eastern
bluebird
nesting box

As a child growing up in rural southwestern Ohio, I very rarely saw bluebirds. The times when I did catch a glimpse of blue darting around, it was more likely an indigo bunting and not a bluebird. The reason was that insecticides and a few terrible blizzards had taken their toll on these colorful creatures. It was not until many years later that the bluebird population increased to a point where now I normally have at least three or four nesting pairs, and I see them diving down to the ground for insects quite regularly.

This bluebird house is based on a traditional design that's been in use for decades. It utilizes a removable top for inspection and cleaning, and is fairly straightforward to construct. The only tricky part is cutting the dado for the roof, a process that is made easier if you have access to a table saw. This version is made from poplar with thin strips of cherry for accent, though almost any weather-resistant softwood could be used.

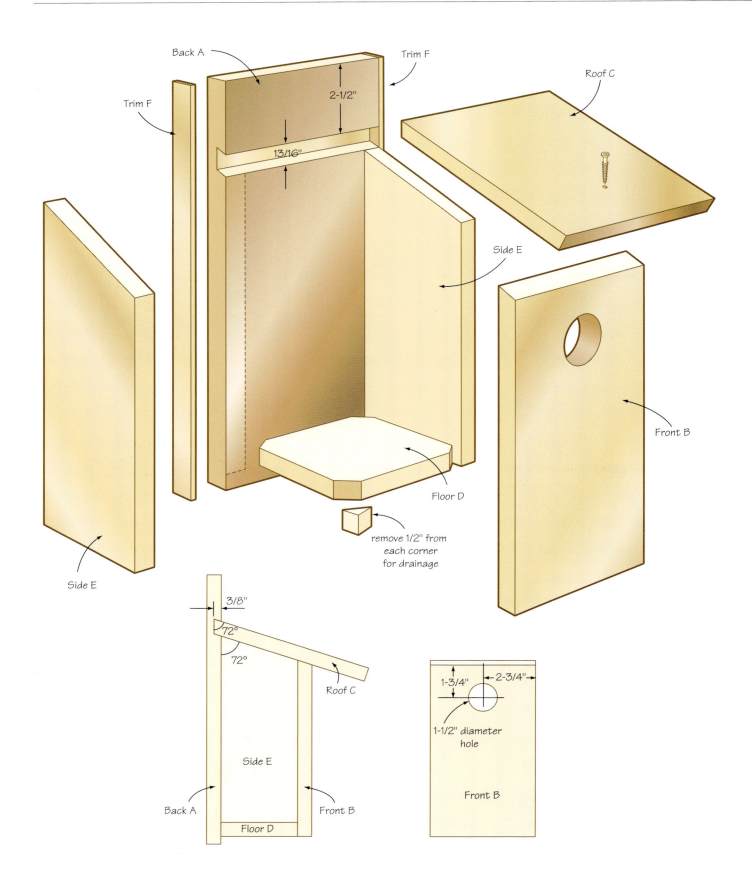

Back A

Trim F

Trim F

2-1/2"

13/16"

Trim F

Roof C

Side E

Front B

Floor D

remove 1/2" from
each corner
for drainage

Side E

3/8"

72°

72°

Roof C

Side E

Back A

Front B

Floor D

1-3/4"

2-3/4"

1-1/2" diameter
hole

Front B

eastern bluebird nesting box

Schedule of Materials: **EASTERN BLUEBIRD NESTING BOX**

LETTER	QUANTITY	PART	STOCK	THICKNESS	WIDTH	LENGTH	COMMENTS
A	1	Back	1×6	¾	5½	14½	
B	1	Front	1×6	¾	5½	9½	Center a 1½" hole 1¾" from top.
C	1	Roof	1×8	¾	5½	8½	
D	1	Floor	1×6	¾	4	4	Cut ½" each corner for drainage.
E	2	Sides	1×6	¾	4	10½	Cut top edge at a 18° angle.
F	2	Trim	Cherry	⅛	¾	14½	

Hardware and Supplies
- 1⅝" galvanized screws
- Waterproof polyurethane glue

vital statistics

Eastern Bluebird
(*Sialia sialus*)

SIZE:
7"

NUMBER OF EGGS:
4 or 5

LENGTH OF INCUBATION:
14 days

BROODS PER SEASON:
Usually 2

FOOD:
Insects and spiders, fruits, berries and seeds

RANGE:
Summer, central to eastern United States north to Canada; winter, southern United States west to Texas

About the Eastern Bluebird

The eastern bluebird is a member of the thrush family, just like the robin. Bluebirds nest almost exclusively in cavities made by other birds, such as abandoned woodpecker holes. But due to extensive deforestation, they have adapted quite well to the use of nesting boxes.

Bluebirds fly north in the early spring, and tend to return to the area in which they nested previously. If this is their first return, they will usually choose a site near where they hatched. First come the males to stake out their territory, and then come the females. Once the eggs are laid, the female remains on the nest up to 4 days after the hatching, as newly hatched bluebirds are not capable of producing their own heat. Both mother and father, after that period, share in the feeding duties. Once the fledglings leave the nesting box, the father usually stays close by and continues to feed the young for several more weeks until they are strong enough to fend for themselves.

House Placement

Bluebirds require semi-open land. They really don't prefer the suburbs, so rural locations are going to be the most successful. Generally, areas where there is at least on acre of open land are going to be the most acceptable sites for houses. Grass and hayfields, meadows, lawns and especially old apple orchards make the best locations. Fencerows are also ideal, as the males love to sit on top of the posts and sing to set out their territory.

The boxes themselves can be mounted in a variety of ways. The easiest way, and the one I've found most successful, is to mount the box directly to the old fence posts, if you are lucky enough to have a location that includes such structures. Metal fence posts placed solely for mounting purposes have also worked well for me. Dead trees with sound wood also make an ideal location.

Mount the boxes 4 to 6 feet off the ground, and if possible, place the box so that the entrance faces open land, away from road traffic. Consider installing predator guards on any posts to keep the nests safe and secure.

1 | MEASURE AND MARK
Lay out the dimensions of your pieces using a combination square (or ruler) and pencil. If you lay out all the pieces at once, remember to allow room for the saw blade kerf.

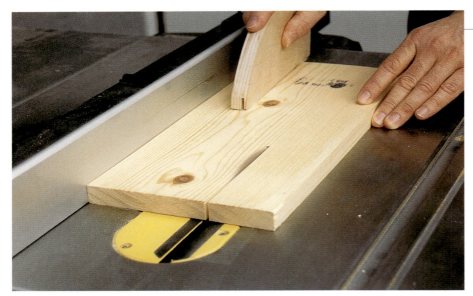

2

CUT TO SIZE

Cut the pieces to size as indicated in the Schedule of Materials. There are many ways to do this — here I'm using a table saw. You could just as easily use a jigsaw or circular saw.

3

MARK AND CUT THE SIDES

Take each side and mark an 18° wedge starting at one corner on top edge (to allow for the slope of the roof). With the saw of your choice, cut the section away.

4

MARK AND DRILL THE ENTRANCE HOLE LOCATION

On the front piece, measure down the center of the board 1³⁄₄" from the top. Mark this spot with your pencil, as that will be the location of the center of the entrance hole. With your hole cutter or Forstner bit, drill the entrance hole.

5

ADD FLOOR DRAINAGE

Mark and remove $1/2$" from each corner to allow for drainage.

things to look out for

Tree swallows also prefer this type of nest box. But since tree swallows are extremely territorial, simply mount two boxes within 15 to 20 feet of each other. That way, you're sure to have one available for bluebirds.

Bluebird nests are very vulnerable to predation, especially if fence posts are used as mounting surfaces. Make sure you use some sort of predator guard to help protect the nest.

Blowflies also are a real problem for bluebirds. The larvae attach themselves to newly hatched birds and suck away the nestlings' blood. Inspect regularly for blowfly larvae, and don't be afraid to pick up the nestlings in your efforts — it's an old wives' tale that a nestling touched by human hands will be abandoned by its mother. Also lift up the nest itself to make sure that there are no larvae hiding in the darkness of the nesting material.

6 | **BEVEL THE ROOF**

Set your table saw to an 18° bevel, and remove the back edge of the roof as shown here.

7 | SAND

With your sander or sandpaper, remove any loose bits or splinters that may be in the way during assembly.

8 | THE COMPLETED PIECES

When you have cut and sanded the pieces, you'll have a collection of parts that looks like this.

9 | CUT THE DADO

The roof on this bluebird house fits into a groove, or dado, on the back. To mark the location for the dado, take the back piece and draw a line across the width 2½" down from the top. Then draw a second line ¾" below the first, thus indicating the placement for the dado. Set the blade angle at 18°, and set the blade depth at ⅜" on your table saw. Cut across the width of the back, starting at the bottom edge mark you just made. Once you've made the first cut, move the fence ⅛" closer to the blade, and make a second cut just above the first. Continue with this process until you have a series of cuts running between the drawn edges of the dado.

eastern bluebird nesting box

10

ATTACH A SIDE

Now it's time to attach the first side. With a damp cloth, slightly moisten the back where the first side will be glued, starting at the bottom edge of the dado. Apply polyurethane glue to the back edge of the side, line up the top point of the side with the bottom edge of the dado, and attach with screws. Then use 1⅝" galvanized screws to finish securing the side to the back.

11

ATTACH THE OTHER SIDE

Repeat the process for the opposite side, attaching with screws.

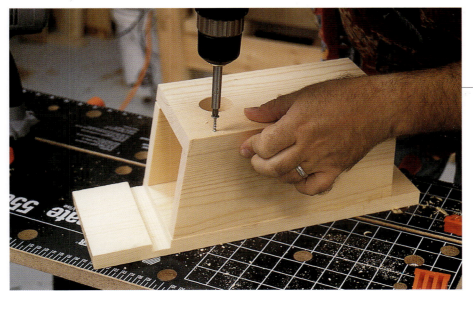

12

ATTACH THE FRONT

Once the second side has cured, attach the front in the same manner.

13

ATTACH THE BOTTOM

Glue the bottom in place. Use a hammer to tap the floor into position.

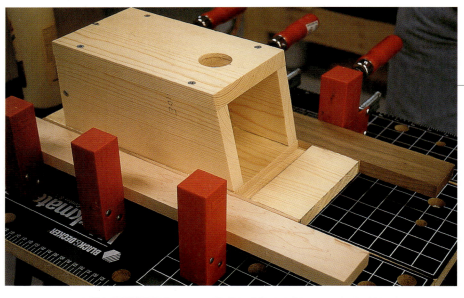

14

ATTACH THE SIDE TRIM

I used thin ¹/₈"-thick cherry strips down the sides of the back to provide both decoration and side stops for the dado (that way the roof won't slide back and forth once fitted in place). Apply glue and clamp the side strips in place.

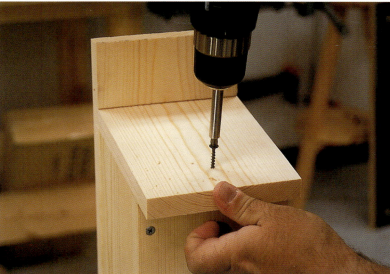

15

ATTACH THE ROOF

Slip the back edge of the roof into the dado in the back piece, and secure the front edge with a screw. Finally, sand everything down, and the nesting box is ready to use!

eastern bluebird nesting box

predator guards

Bluebird nest boxes can be vulnerable to predation, especially if mounted on old fence posts that are easily climbed by animals. To keep the nests safe, use some form of predator guard. I've used different types of guards over the years, and while none is perfect, I've found these four to work rather well at protecting the nest.

The first type is called a baffle block, and it is perhaps the simplest form of protection. A baffle block is nothing more than an extension of the entrance hole. The baffle block makes it difficult for raccoons to reach in and grab eggs or nestlings (see drawing 1). A version I've seen of this idea includes mounting a section of copper pipe in the opening. By adding the pipe, you make it next to impossible for squirrels or other gnawing animals to attempt to enlarge the opening.

Next is a wire guard, which works very well against cats. Basically a perimeter of $\frac{1}{2}$" galvanized wire mesh, the wire guard creates a sharp barrier that neither cats nor raccoons like to cross (see drawing 2).

Third, and one of my personal favorites, is the cone baffle. Made from a circle of metal, the cone baffle works great keeping snakes away from nests. Use the cone baffle where small-diameter mounting posts are being used, as it is rather difficult to mount this type of guard to a living tree (see drawing 3).

Finally, there is a sleeve guard. Made from either plastic or metal, the sleeve also works great at keeping raccoons, cats and snakes at bay (see drawing 4).

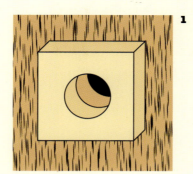

1

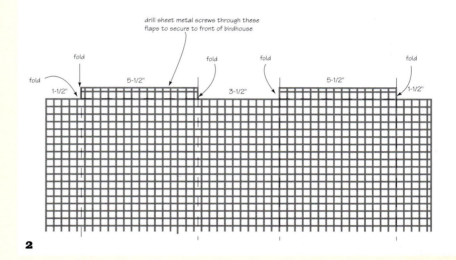

drill sheet metal screws through these flaps to secure to front of birdhouse

fold   fold   fold   fold

fold   5-1/2"   3-1/2"   5-1/2"   fold

1-1/2"   1-1/2"

2

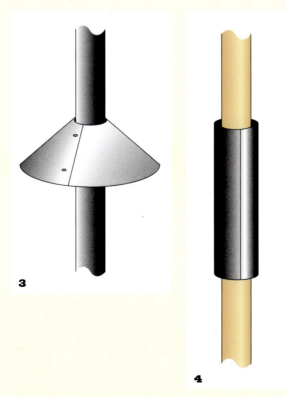

3

4

peterson bluebird house

Bluebirds have almost as many choices for houses as humans do. There are many designs out there, and each has its own unique benefits. The Olson, Bauldry, Lake, PVC, Flip Flop, NABS, Slot and Open Top are all designs that are used in different parts of the country with varying success. In fact, there's so much research on bluebirds alone that I could have written a book solely on bluebird nest boxes!

The box design shown here, called the Peterson or Wedge Box, has been used quite successfully throughout the north-central United States. It has a unique triangular shape, small floor and oval-shaped entrance hole. There has been some research that indicates bluebirds may indeed prefer the smaller floor space. The downside of this design, in my opinion, is that the larger entrance hole can be used by starlings, a species that you definitely do not want to encourage. So if you decide to go with this design, keep a sharp eye out that the nest box inhabitants are indeed the ones you want, and not some uninvited intruder.

This design is substantially harder to construct than the simple box in project 3. Power tools are almost necessary here, though with patience and a steady hand you could get by without them. Pay particular attention to the angles when cutting the pieces. I built the example here from pine, though rough-cut cedar would be an even better choice.

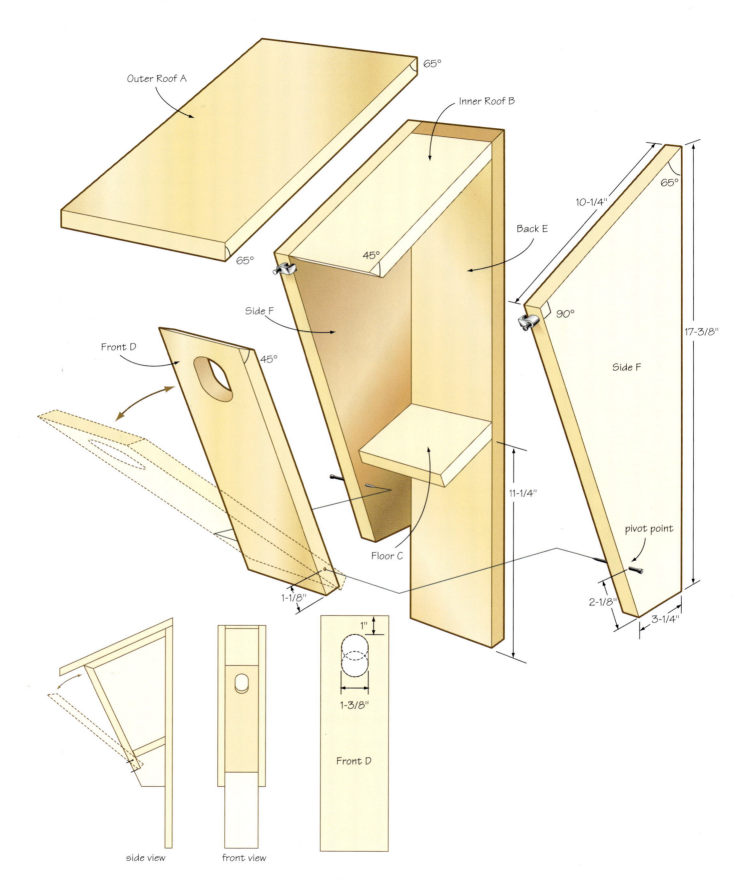

Outer Roof A

65°

Inner Roof B

65°

Back E

65°

10-1/4"

45°

Side F

Side F

90°

17-3/8"

Front D

45°

11-1/4"

Floor C

pivot point

1-1/8"

2-1/8"

3-1/4"

1"

1-3/8"

Front D

side view

front view

peterson bluebird house

Schedule of Materials: PETERSON BLUEBIRD HOUSE

LETTER	QUANTITY	PART	STOCK	THICKNESS	WIDTH	LENGTH	COMMENTS
A	1	Outer Roof	1×12	$3/4$	$9^{1}/_{4}$	13	
B	1	Inner Roof	1×12	$3/4$	$3^{1}/_{2}$	$10^{1}/_{4}$	Cut ends at 45° & 65°.
C	1	Floor	1×12	$3/4$	$3^{1}/_{2}$	3	Cut one end at 65°.
D	1	Front	1×12	$3/4$	$3^{1}/_{2}$	$12^{1}/_{2}$	Cut top end at 45°.
E	1	Back	1×12	$3/4$	$3^{1}/_{2}$	24	Cut top end at 65°.
F	2	Sides	1×12	$3/4$	$10^{1}/_{4}$	$20^{3}/_{8}$	Rough dimensions; see illustration.

Hardware and Supplies

• $1^{1}/_{2}$" galvanized finishing nails

• Audiovisual cable stays

• Waterproof glue

1

MEASURE OUT THE PARTS

Make all your measurements based on the illustration and Schedule of Materials. Be especially careful when making your measurements to allow for the various angles involved in this design. Remember that the inner roof needs to be cut at 45° at one end and 65° at the other. The outer roof needs to be cut at 65° at both ends. The front needs to be cut to a 45° angle at the top edge. The floor needs to be cut at a 65° angle at the back edge, and the back piece needs to be cut to a 65° angle at the top edge.

2

CUT OUT THE PIECES

After carefully taking all your measurements, cut out the pieces, remembering to allow for the kerf of the saw blade. Pay careful attention when cutting the sides. You can start with rough blanks of $10^{1}/_{4}$" × $20^{3}/_{8}$", and then make the final dimensional cuts based on the dimensions shown in the illustration.

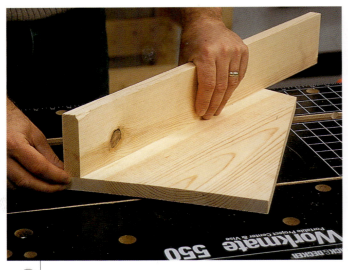

3 | ATTACH ONE SIDE

Once you have all the pieces cut to size, start the construction by attaching the left side to the back piece using waterproof glue.

4 | ATTACH THE INNER ROOF

Next, glue the inner roof to both the back and the left side.

5 | ATTACH THE FLOOR

Mount the floor 10½" below the inner roof's top edge, gluing it to the left side and the back.

6 | ATTACH THE RIGHT SIDE

Once the glue is dry on the inner roof and the floor, mount the right side to the assembly.

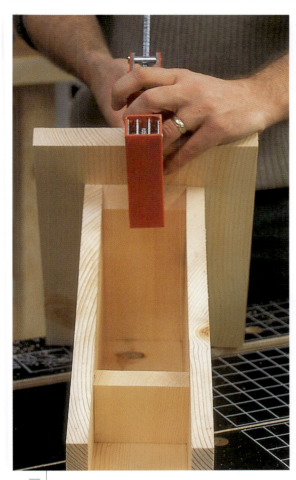

7 | **ATTACH THE OUTER ROOF**

Glue the outer roof to the inner roof and edges of the sides and back. Then set the assembly aside to allow the glue to cure.

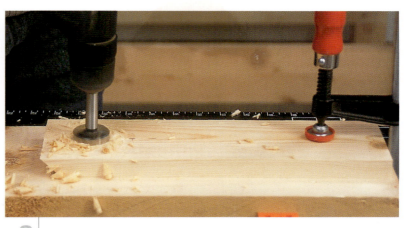

8 | **BEGIN THE ENTRANCE HOLE**

Begin to form the oval entrance hole by locating a $1\frac{3}{8}$"-wide hole 1" below the top edge of the front piece.

9 | **DRILL THE SECOND HOLE**

Locate another $1\frac{3}{8}$"-wide hole so that its bottom edge is $2\frac{1}{4}$" down from the top edge of the hole you just drilled in the previous step.

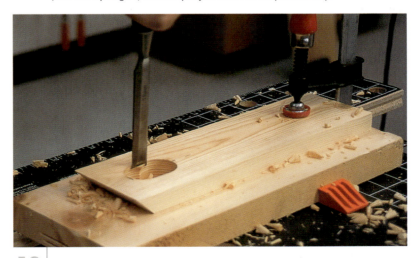

10 | **CLEAN OUT THE WASTE AND MOUNT THE FRONT**

Once the two overlapping holes are drilled, clean out the waste between them with a chisel. Then mount the front to the assembly by driving a $1\frac{1}{2}$" finishing nail through the sides and into the edge of the front piece. Locate these nails 2" up from the bottom edge of each side. Drive in the audiovisual cable stays to secure the front, sand everything down, and the birdhouse is finished.

wood duck
nesting box

The wood duck is another one of those species that I didn't see much of as a child. Though I grew up very close to the banks of one of southern Ohio's largest rivers, the Great Miami, the only ducks I saw with any regularity were mallards. I'm happy to say that the situation has greatly improved. Wood ducks are a common sight now, not just there but across most of the United States. Once close to extinction, the wood duck has made a spectacular recovery, and is now one of the most common waterfowl species.

This nesting box is very easy to construct. There are a few unique features, such as the oval entrance hole and the exit ladder inside; nevertheless, it's pretty straightforward. My example is built of pine, and for a reason. Over the years, I've found that these nesting boxes take quite a beating. Because of harsh weather, water from ponds, the comings and goings of the wood duck itself, and overly curious muskrat and other wildlife, these boxes almost always need repairing or replacement each year. For that reason, I used a less-expensive lumber in construction.

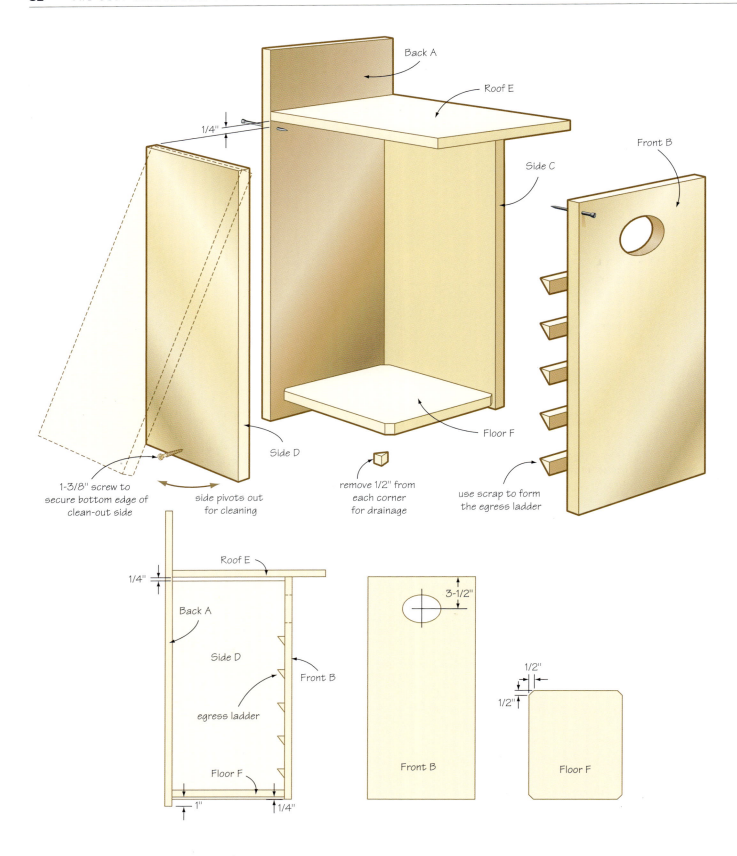

Back A

Roof E

1/4"

Side C

Front B

Side D

1-3/8" screw to
secure bottom edge of
clean-out side

side pivots out
for cleaning

remove 1/2" from
each corner
for drainage

use scrap to form
the egress ladder

Floor F

Roof E

1/4"

Back A

Side D

Front B

egress ladder

Floor F

1"   1/4"

3-1/2"

Front B

1/2"

1/2"

Floor F

wood duck nesting box

Schedule of Materials: **WOOD DUCK NESTING BOX**

LETTER	QUANTITY	PART	STOCK	THICKNESS	WIDTH	LENGTH	COMMENTS
A	1	Back	1×12	3/4	11 1/4	32	
B	1	Front	1×12	3/4	11 1/4	24	Cut entrance hole per illustration.
C	1	Side	1×12	3/4	11 1/4	24	
D	1	Side	1×12	3/4	11 1/4	23 3/4	This side shorter to allow for pivoting.
E	1	Top	1×12	3/4	11 1/4	16	
F	1	Bottom	1×12	3/4	11 1/4	9 3/4	Cut 1/2" from each corner for drainage.

Hardware and Supplies

• 1 5/8" galvanized screws

• 2" stainless steel ringshank nails

• Waterproof glue

vital statistics

Wood Duck
(Aix sponsa)

SIZE:
18" to 20"

NUMBER OF EGGS:
Usually 10 to 12

LENGTH OF INCUBATION:
Approximately 30 days

BROODS PER SEASON:
1 or 2

FOOD:
Seeds, fruits, small aquatic and terrestrial animals

RANGE:
Summer, north to lower Canada; winter, south to Texas; year-round, Atlantic Coast west to the Mississippi River

About the Wood Duck

Wood ducks are secondary cavity nesters. This means that they do not make their own cavities as woodpeckers do — they search for an abandoned hole or naturally-occurring cavity in which to built their nests.

Wood ducks prefer more cover than many other species of ducks. They like locations that are made up of flooded shrubs and trees with small areas of open water. If you live up North and are lucky enough to be near beaver ponds, then you've got the ideal wood duck environment already custom-made for you. They also prefer areas where the water level is stable and not prone to constant rising or falling.

Wood ducks do not build nests per se. Since they are secondary cavity nesters, they traditionally rely on materials left behind by the previous owner of the cavity. It's not until the female has about half of her eggs laid that she begins to add any material to the nest, and then it's simply feathers plucked out of her own breast. Because of this nesting behavior, it is very important to fill the nest box with from 3" to 6" of wood chips or shavings.

But a word of warning — do not use cedar shavings or chips. Cedar produces an oil that is released through chips or shavings, and this oil can be irritating to both the skin and the respiratory system of the duck (the same holds true for household pets).

House Placement

Nest boxes for wood ducks should be placed a minimum of 4 feet off the water's surface or 6 feet off of dry ground. Wood ducks also seem to prefer boxes that are either mounted directly over water or set back about 50 feet from it. For some reason, they don't take as well to nest boxes mounted directly at the water's edge. Since wood ducks are not territorial animals, you can place boxes as close together as 50 feet. Look for areas where there are nut- or berry-producing trees, as the fruit from them make up the bulk of the adult wood duck diet.

1 | **MEASURE AND CUT**

Measure out each piece for your wood duck nesting box as per the Schedule of Materials and illustration, and cut to size. Remember to allow for the kerf of the saw blade, and to make one side a 1/4" shorter than the other to allow for both ventilation and for the hinging motion.

things to look out for

All sorts of other critters like to use wood duck boxes as homes. Hooded mergansers, starlings, squirrels, field mice and even honeybees have all been known to use these boxes.

Raccoons, snakes, mink, foxes, owls and turtles are all dangers for young wood ducks. Deeper boxes can keep some egg-grabbing predators at bay, so experiment with deeper designs if your predation situation calls for it.

2

ALLOW FOR DRAINAGE
Cut ½" off each corner of the bottom to allow for drainage.

3

BEGIN THE ENTRANCE HOLE
First, draw a 3" circle centered 3½" down from the top of the front. Then draw two 1" circles centered on opposite edges of the 3" circle you just drew. Then take your hole saw and cut the 3" opening.

4

DRILL THE SIDES OF THE ENTRANCE HOLE
Now drill out the 1" holes you previously marked.

5 | FINISH THE ENTRANCE HOLE

Clean out the waste between the holes with either your jigsaw or a chisel. You'll be left with an entrance hole that is 3" × 4".

6 | ADD THE LADDER

It's necessary to add some form of climbing system that allows the young ducklings to get out of the box once they hatch. I've had great success by building a ladder from scrap bits of wood. Other options would include ¼" wire or plastic mesh. But to use scrap wood, simply take any small stock (here I've used triangular bits that were left over after I beveled the edges of other birdhouse projects) and cut it down to 3" to 4" in length. I don't run the ladder all the way to the bottom, as I know I'll be filling in the last six inches with wood chips. Glue the scraps in a row up towards the entrance hole to create a ladder-like progression. If you opt for wire or plastic mesh, merely staple it in place.

7 | ATTACH ONE SIDE

Mount the right side to the back board using 1⅝" screws and glue.

ATTACH THE FRONT

Next, mount the front to the right side, again using 1⁵⁄₈" screws and glue.

9 | **ATTACH THE HINGING SIDE**

Align the left side flush with the bottom edge of the front. Clamp together and drive in 2" stainless steel ringshank nails 2" down from the top edge to serve as hinges. I like using the heavier ringshank nails with this nesting box, as I have found they hold better in the wetland environment than finishing nails.

10 | **ATTACH THE BOTTOM**

Mount the bottom to the nest box assembly using 1⁵⁄₈" screws and glue.

wood duck nesting box

11
SECURE THE HINGING SIDE
Rather than use the audiovisual cable stays as we have in other projects, drill in a $1\frac{5}{8}$" screw to secure the hinging side. Again, I prefer the heavier hardware here because of the wetland environment.

12 | ATTACH THE ROOF
Using $1\frac{5}{8}$" screws and glue, attach the roof to the nest box assembly. Make sure you get a good waterproof seal all around the top — don't be stingy with the glue!

13 | SAND
Once the assembly is finished and the glue has cured, sand everything down, and your project is completed!

northern flicker
nesting box

Woodpeckers of every type have always fascinated me. Their energy and industrious nature never cease to amaze me. And except for those rare times when a well-meaning woodpecker decided to hammer on my roof on an early weekend morning, I always delight in their presence.

This nest box is designed for the northern flicker, one of the larger woodpeckers in North America. The box is built from Douglas fir, and is very simple to construct. In fact, about the only problem you may have is figuring out a way to mount the nesting box up high enough, since flickers like to be about 20 feet off the ground!

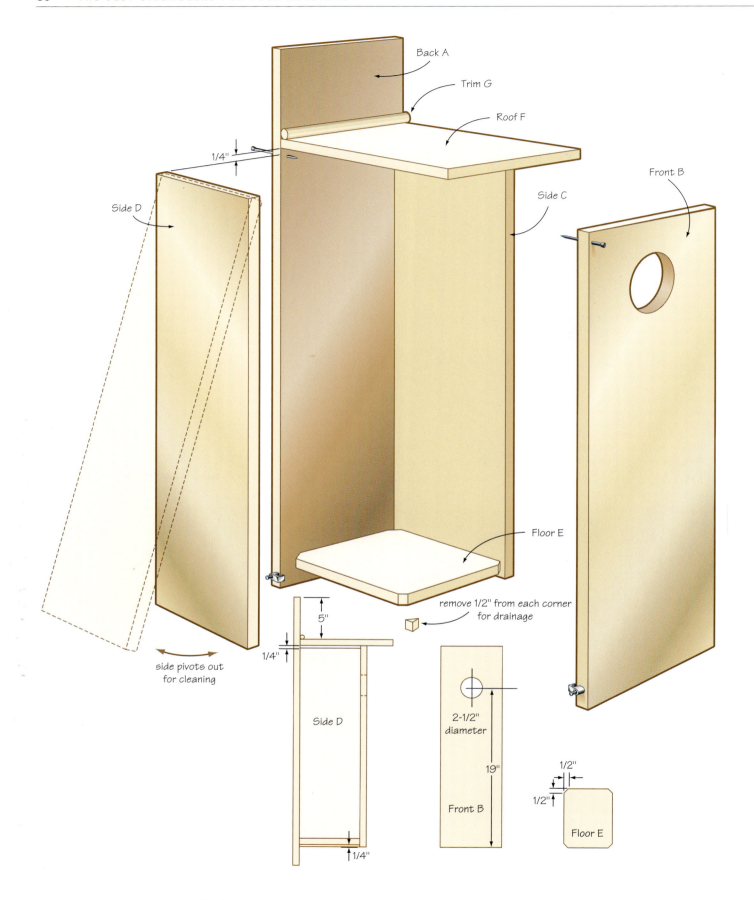

Back A

Trim G

Roof F

Front B

Side D

1/4"

Side C

Floor E

side pivots out
for cleaning

5"

1/4"

Side D

1/4"

remove 1/2" from each corner
for drainage

2-1/2"
diameter

19"

Front B

1/2"

1/2"

Floor E

northern flicker nesting box

Schedule of Materials: **NORTHERN FLICKER NESTING BOX**

LETTER	QUANTITY	PART	STOCK	THICKNESS	WIDTH	LENGTH	COMMENTS
A	1	Back	1x8	3/4	7 1/8	32	
B	1	Front	1x8	3/4	7 1/8	24	
C	1	Side	1x8	3/4	7	24	
D	1	Side	1x8	3/4	7	23 3/4	
E	1	Floor	1x8	3/4	5 5/8	7	
F	1	Roof	1x8	3/4	7 1/8	10 3/4	
G	1	Trim	Dowel	1/2 dia.		7 1/8	

Hardware and Supplies
- 1 5/8" galvanized screws
- Audiovisual cable stays
- 2" stainless steel ringshank nails
- Waterproof glue

About the Northern Flicker

The northern flicker is a large and colorful woodpecker. It is a primary cavity nester, meaning that it generally uses cavities that it makes itself. Because so many other birds use the flicker's old homes as nesting sites, it is an extremely important bird to have around.

Most woodpeckers are known for their hammering on trees in search of insects. And while the flicker does partake in this behavior, it is most known for hunting on the ground in search of ants. It has a long, sticky tongue that it uses to slurp up ants wherever it can find them.

There are several subspecies of flickers, and all of them will use this type of nesting box, though they prefer to excavate their own nests. The yellow-shafted flicker is more common in the East, though its numbers have been in decline due mostly to deforestation and competition with the dreaded European starling. The red-shafted flicker is more common in the West, and has also been in decline from the same factors. The gilded flicker inhabits the deserts of the Southwest.

House Placement

The best place for a flicker nesting box is in semi-open country or light woodlands. Sunny locations work well, and my experience has shown the higher it is mounted, the better. Technically, anywhere from 6 to 20 feet is the placement you're after, but I have had much better luck in the upper end of that range than I have in the lower. Mount the box to a dead tree where a flicker would normally be attracted. Before mounting, tightly pack the interior of the nesting box with wood chips, sawdust and shavings so that the bird will think it is excavating a dead tree (remember to stay away from cedar shavings or chips as they can be harmful to wildlife).

vital statistics

Northern Flicker
(Colaptes auratus)

SIZE:
12" to 14"

NUMBER OF EGGS:
Usually 5 to 8
(but as many as 12)

LENGTH OF INCUBATION:
11 to 14 days

BROODS PER SEASON:
Usually 1

FOOD:
Mostly insects and larvae; seeds, nuts and suet in the winter.

RANGE:
Summer, north to Alaska; Winter, south to Mexico; year-round, continental United States

things to look out for

Many species give the flicker a run for its money when it comes to nesting. Keep an eye out for European starlings, squirrels, screech owls and house sparrows.

Once the flicker's eggs are laid, watch out for snakes, raccoons and other predators that would steal and eat them.

Remember to pack the nest box tightly with shavings and wood chips before mounting. That way, the flicker will think it is excavating a rotten tree.

1 MEASURE

Measure out all the parts for your nesting box as indicated in the Schedule of Materials and illustration. Remember to allow for the kerf of the saw blade and to make one side a 1/4" shorter than the other to allow for the pivoting movement.

2 CUT TO LENGTH

Cut out the parts for the nest box based on the measurements you made in Step 1.

3 CUT OUT THE ENTRANCE HOLE

Center and drill out a 2 1/2" entrance hole 19" from the bottom edge of the front piece.

northern flicker nesting box

4

ATTACH ONE SIDE

Attach the right side to the back using 1⅝" galvanized screws and waterproof glue.

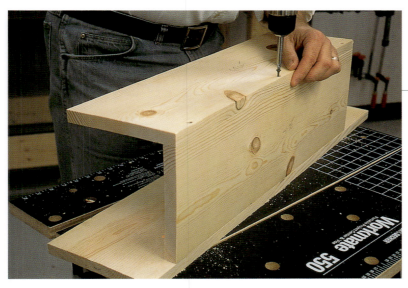

5

ATTACH THE FRONT

In the same manner as in Step 4, attach the front piece to the right side.

6

ATTACH THE OTHER SIDE

Now align the left pivoting side so that it is flush with the bottom edge of the front piece. Clamp together, and drive 2" stainless steel ringshank nails down through the front and back and into the side to serve as pivot points.

7

ALLOW FOR DRAINAGE
Remove ¹/₂" from each corner of the floor to allow for drainage.

8

ATTACH THE FLOOR
Using screws and glue, attach the floor. Once the glue is dry, drive in the audiovisual cable stays to serve as locks for the pivoting side.

northern flicker nesting box

9 | ATTACH THE TOP

Again with glue and galvanized screws, attach the top to the nesting box assembly.

10 | GLUE ON THE TRIM

Run a bead of waterproof glue along where the top meets the back, and press into place a $\frac{1}{2}$"-diameter by $7\frac{1}{8}$"-long dowel to further waterproof the top seam.

11 | SAND

Finally, sand the entire project.

12 | DONE!

The completed northern flicker nesting box.

american
kestrel
nesting box

I remember the first time I saw one of these jeweled beauties. One of my childhood duties was to mow our one-acre lawn. Late one summer afternoon, in the middle of this task, I happened to glance up at the power lines that ran along our road. There, sitting and watching me intently, was an American kestrel (also known as a sparrow hawk). I had never seen one before and was totally confused by its size — I had only seen large birds of prey, like red-tailed hawks and others of the same sort.

I quickly killed the lawn mower and ran inside to grab my Golden bird guide. By the time I came back out, the bird had flown off, but it was easy to find its image in my fieldbook.

Though I've seen this smallest of our hawks countless times since, I still get a thrill whenever I see its wonderful colors flash by in pursuit of some elusive prey.

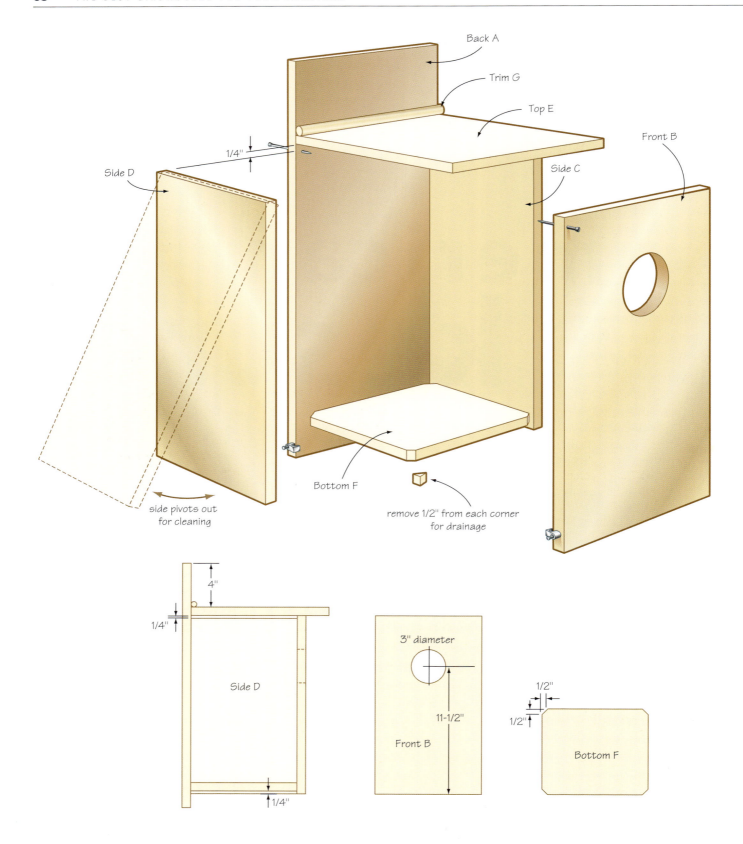

Back A

Trim G

Top E

Front B

Side D

Side C

1/4"

side pivots out
for cleaning

Bottom F

remove 1/2" from each corner
for drainage

4"

1/4"

Side D

1/4"

3" diameter

11-1/2"

Front B

1/2"

1/2"

Bottom F

american kestrel nesting box

Schedule of Materials: **AMERICAN KESTREL NESTING BOX**

LETTER	QUANTITY	PART	STOCK	THICKNESS	WIDTH	LENGTH	COMMENTS
A	I	Back	1×10	$3/4$	$9^1/4$	22	
B	I	Front	1×10	$3/4$	$9^1/4$	16	Center a 3" hole $11^1/2$" from bottom.
C	I	Side	1×10	$3/4$	$9^1/4$	16	Drill two $1/4$" holes for ventilation.
D	I	Side	1×10	$3/4$	$9^1/4$	$15^3/4$	$1/4$" difference allows for pivoting.
E	I	Top	1×10	$3/4$	$9^1/4$	12	
F	I	Bottom	1×10	$3/4$	$9^1/4$	$7^3/4$	Remove $1/2$" on corners for drainage.
G	I	Trim	Dowel	$1/2$ dia.		$9^1/4$	

Hardware and Supplies
- $1^5/8$" galvanized screws
- Audiovisual cable stays
- 2" stainless steel ringshank nails
- Waterproof glue

About the American Kestrel

The smallest and most social of North America's hawks, this beautiful little bird is also our only cavity-nesting hawk. They feed primarily on small mammals, such as mice, voles and insects (especially grasshoppers). They have also been known to feed on small birds (like house sparrows), which is how they earned the colloquial name of "sparrow hawk." More common in the past than it is now, its numbers took a dive in no small part due to the use of insecticides such as DDT.

House Placement

American Kestrels prefer the open country, though they'll live just about anywhere if their choices are limited. Ideally, look for grasslands, meadows or abandoned fields for ideal house placement, as these areas are most likely to attract their preferred food source, small mammals.

When looking for a house site, find a location that includes at least 1 acre of open land. That way, this little hawk will have adequate hunting range. If possible, place the nest box near trees with dead limbs, telephone poles or other structures where the bird can sit high to watch for a meal.

Mount the house at least 10 feet above the ground, and make sure there is a clear-cut area in front of the opening to allow for a flyway. Once mounted, and at the beginning of each nesting season, fill the box with 1" to 2" of wood chips or shavings (but don't use cedar, as it can be harmful to wildlife).

vital statistics

American Kestrel
(Falco sparverius)

SIZE:
2" to 9"

NUMBER OF EGGS:
As many as 7, but usually 4 or 5

LENGTH OF INCUBATION:
Approximately 30 days

BROODS PER SEASON:
Usually I

FOOD:
Insects, mice (and other small mammals), small snakes and frogs

RANGE:
Summer, as far north as upper Canada and lower Alaska, throughout the Continental United States; winter, South to Panama; year-round, areas of the temperate Midwest, including the eastern seaboard across to the Pacific coast

1

MEASURE
Measure off all the parts based on the dimensions in the Schedule of Materials and the illustration. Remember to allow for the saw kerf, and to make one side a $1/4$" shorter than the other to allow for the pivoting movement.

CUT TO SIZE
Cut your parts to size according to the measurements you made in Step 1.

ALLOW FOR DRAINAGE
Remove ¹/₂" from each corner of the bottom to allow for proper drainage.

things to look out for

Starlings love to take over just about any nest box, so be sure to evict any that start to show interest.

Gray squirrels and screech owls also love these boxes, so check often to make sure that you don't have an unwelcome tenant. Don't attempt to inspect the nest until two weeks after the kestrel eggs are laid, as the mother may abandon the clutch if it is disturbed too early.

CUT THE HOLE
Cut out a 3"-diameter entrance hole centered 11¹/₂" up from the bottom edge of the front piece.

american kestrel nesting box

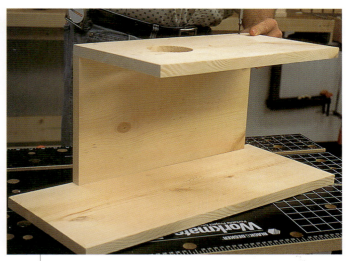

5 | **ATTACH ONE SIDE**
Using $1^5/_8$" screws and waterproof glue, attach the right side onto the back piece. Align the side so that its bottom edge is 2" from the bottom edge of the back piece.

6 | **ATTACH THE FRONT**
In the same manner as you used to attach the side, attach the front piece onto the nest box assembly.

7

ATTACH THE OTHER SIDE
Align the left pivoting side so that its bottom edge is flush with the front piece. Clamp together, and drive 2" stainless steel ringshank nails through both the front and back to serve as pivot points. Make sure the nails are in line with each other, or the side will not pivot properly.

8 | **ATTACH THE BOTTOM**

Attach the bottom to the nest box assembly using $1\frac{5}{8}$" galvanized screws and waterproof glue. Make sure you align the bottom so that it sits approximately $\frac{1}{2}$" in from the bottom edges of the four walls.

9 | **ADD THE LOCKS**

Drive in two audiovisual cable stays to serve as locks for the pivoting side.

10

ADD THE TOP

Using glue and screws, attach the top to the back, right side and front piece.

american kestrel nesting box

11 | **ADD TRIM**

Run a bead of waterproof glue along the juncture of the roof and back piece, and press into it a $\frac{1}{2}$"-diameter × $9\frac{1}{4}$" dowel rod. By adding this piece, you make the box that much more waterproof.

12 | **SAND**

With either an electric sander or sandpaper, smooth out your project.

13

COMPLETED

The finished American Kestrel nesting box.

barred
owl
nesting box

Owls have been associated with the mysterious and supernatural for centuries. Perhaps because of their large eyes, which give them a wise, all-knowing appearance, or perhaps from their nocturnal behavior, owls have been both revered and feared. I, myself, delight in spotting owls. I remember one particular barred owl, however, that proved quite difficult to find. I was hiking in a particularly dense part of forest one early fall evening when I heard the barred owl's distinctive call. Assuming I could follow the sound to its roosting place, I took off through the forest, but every time I got within camera range, the owl would take wing and move further into the trees. After about a mile of this game of tag, I gave up and wandered back to my campsite.

The barred owl nesting box here is built from pine. And because of its large opening, I chose not to incorporate a pivoting clean-out side. This project is very straightforward and quite simple to construct. A unique feature of it is that the entrance is on the side of the box rather than the front — a feature that the owls in my area seem to prefer.

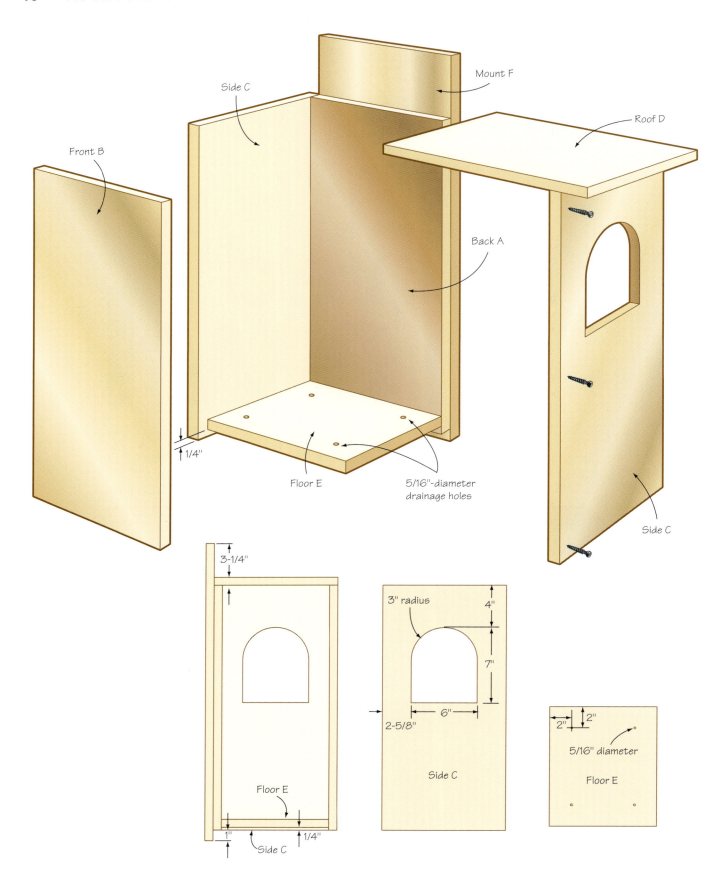

Side C

Mount F

Front B

Roof D

Back A

1/4"

Floor E

5/16"-diameter drainage holes

Side C

3-1/4"

Floor E

1"

Side C

1/4"

3" radius

4"

7"

6"

2-5/8"

Side C

2"

2"

5/16" diameter

Floor E

barred owl nesting box

Schedule of Materials: **BARRED OWL NESTING BOX**

LETTER	QUANTITY	PART	STOCK	THICKNESS	WIDTH	LENGTH	COMMENTS
A	1	Back	1×12	$3/4$	$11^1/4$	23	
B	1	Front	1×12	$3/4$	$11^1/4$	23	
C	2	Sides	1×12	$3/4$	$11^1/4$	23	
D	1	Roof	1×12	$3/4$	$11^1/4$	$14^1/2$	
E	1	Floor	1×12	$3/4$	$9^3/4$	$11^1/4$	Drill four $5/16$" drainage holes.
F	1	Mount	1×12	$3/4$	$11^1/4$	28	

Hardware and Supplies

• $1^5/8$" galvanized screws

• Waterproof glue

About the Barred Owl

Barred owls always give me something to look forward to. Even as early as January, these large owls start their nest-building activities. And when I see them fly, I know I won't have long to wait until the snow starts to melt.

The barred owl is a brown-gray hornless (no ear tufts) owl with white spots on the back, white streaks on the belly that run lengthwise, and white bars, from which its name is derived, on the neck and breast that run crosswise. Its eyes are brown rather than the more common yellow, and it has a wingspan of 3½ to 4 feet.

Generally, barred owls live in larger tracts of deciduous forests, ranging from wet areas, such as wooded swamps, poorly drained woodlots and protected hillsides, to drier, upland area. Recent research indicates that the preference for wetter sites is because these are areas less likely to have been disturbed, particularly by timber activities that remove the mature, deteriorating trees used for nesting sites, rather than a need for water. The presence of a suitable number of mature trees capable of providing perching and nesting cover are crucial for barred owl habitat. Pine groves are frequently used as roosting cover for this species.

The barred owl is a highly vocal owl. It is so loud and noisy that it can be quite easy to find. Its standard call is a series of hoots that sound like someone slowly saying, "who-cooks-for-you, who-cooks-for-you-all." This owl makes many other vocalizations which range from a short yelp or bark to a frenzied and raucous monkey-like squall that can raise the hair on the back of your neck.

Owlets will open their eyes at one week of age and leave the nest at about 30 days of age, but are not fledged until seven to nine weeks of age. After they leave the nest cavity, the young will typically roost on a tree branch, which is oftentimes reached by climbing, until they can fly. The young barred owl climbs trees by grasping the bark of the tree with its beak and talons, flapping its wings then letting go with the beak, quickly stretching its neck out and grabbing onto the bark with its beak again, and pulling and/or walking itself up the tree.

Barred owls rarely build their own nests. Instead, frequently they will use hollow tree cavities such as old hawk, squirrel and crow nests. Barred owl nests are flimsy and poorly constructed, and eggs deposited in them frequently roll out, breaking on impact. This is just one reason why nesting boxes can play a vital role in barred owl conservation.

House Placement

The best place for a barred owl box is about 20 feet up a tree and at least 200 feet away from the nearest human residence. Densely wooded areas can work well, and having water at least within 200 feet also seems to encourage occupancy. And since young owls need a place to perch once they fledge, try to find a site with branches close by the box.

vital statistics

Barred Owl
(Strix varia)

SIZE:
16" to 24"

NUMBER OF EGGS:
uUsually 2 but sometimes as many as 3 or 4

LENGTH OF INCUBATION:
23 to 32 days

BROODS PER SEASON:
1

FOOD:
Mice, wood rats, chipmunks, squirrels, opossums, shrews; wide variety of insects, snakes, lizards, salamanders, crayfish, frogs; occasionally wades in shallow water for fish. Barred owls also like quail, grouse, doves, jays, finches and are known to eat other owls and bats.

RANGE:
Year-round, East Coast west to the Rockies and north into lower Canada

1 MEASURE

Using the Schedule of Materials and illustration, measure out the parts you'll need for construction. Remember to allow for the kerf of the saw blade in your measurements.

2 CUT TO SIZE

Based on the measurements you just made, cut all the pieces to size.

3 DRAW THE ENTRANCE

Create an entrance hole that measures 7" × 6". Start by marking lines at 4" and 11" from the top edge of one of the sides. Then mark lines $2^5/8$" in from the side edges of that same side — this will give you the boundary in which you'll create the opening. Then using a 7" can (or other round object), place its top edge at the 4" line (making sure the saucer is centered between the $2^5/8$" inset boundary lines) and trace a circle around its perimeter. Remember that you're only going to use the top half of this circle — the entrance hole has straight sides that are delineated by those $2^5/8$" inset boundary lines you previously drew.

4 BEGIN THE ENTRANCE

Drill two holes at the junction points of the arc you just drew and the $2^5/8$"-inset boundary lines. The size of the holes is not important — just make sure they are large enough for you to insert the blade of your jigsaw later on. Remember to drill on the inside of the drawn lines, and to have the outer edges of the drill holes just touching the pencil lines.

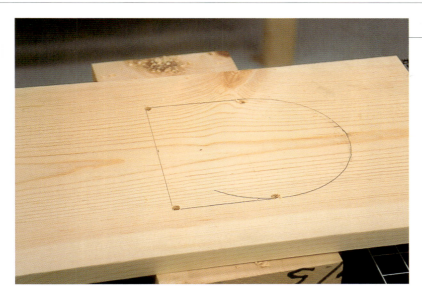

5

DRILL FOR THE BOTTOM OF THE ENTRANCE

Just as you did in Step 4, drill two holes to mark the bottom corners of the entrance hole.

6

CUT OUT THE ENTRANCE

Insert the blade of your jigsaw into one of the holes you drilled and cut around the drawn line of the entrance hole, sort of like a game of connect-the-dots.

7

ATTACH ONE SIDE

Take the side into which you just cut the entrance and attach it to the front using $1\frac{5}{8}$" screws and waterproof glue.

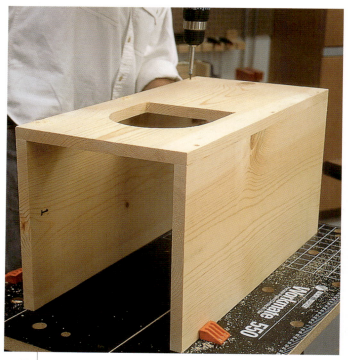

8 | ATTACH THE BACK

In the same manner as in Step 7, attach the back.

9 | ATTACH THE OTHER SIDE

Again in the same manner as in Steps 7 and 8, attach the left side.

10

ATTACH THE ROOF

Using $1\frac{5}{8}$" galvanized screws, attach the roof to the nest-box assembly. Don't use any waterproof glue here, as you may have to remove the roof in the future to discourage squirrels from using the box.

things to look out for

Squirrels like to take over barred owl boxes, so keep a sharp eye out for their presence.

If you find a squirrel has moved in, clear out the box and remove the lid temporarily — squirrels don't like unprotected nesting sites.

Clean out the box once a year, usually in the autumn.

barred owl nesting box

11 | ALLOW FOR DRAINAGE

Draw two lines on the bottom that connect the opposite corners. Measure in 2" on each line and drill four $\frac{5}{16}$" drainage holes.

12 | ATTACH THE FLOOR

Using $1\frac{5}{8}$" galvanized screws and waterproof glue, attach the floor to the nestbox assembly.

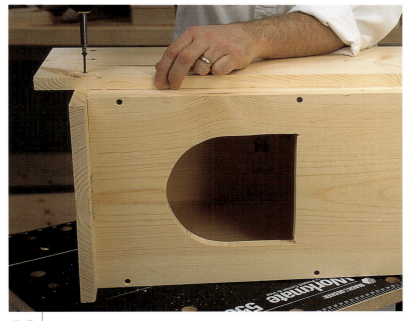

13 | ADD THE MOUNTING BOARD

With $1\frac{5}{8}$" galvanized screws and liberal amounts of waterproof glue, attach the mounting board to the back of the nesting box. Remember that the entrance needs to be on the side.

14 | SAND

Lightly sand your project, add 3" of wood chips in the interior of the box, and it's finished!

purple martin house

Purple martin houses were a common sight when I was a child. Out in the country where I grew up, there were numerous old farmsteads, and just about every one had a martin house somewhere on the property. As a matter of fact, just across my back fence was a farmstead with an old log cabin from before the turn of the century that had been covered over and converted into a more traditional-looking house. The farmstead also had the usual barn, outbuildings, well house and, of course, a martin house. When the day came to tear down the old buildings (as they were becoming terribly unsound), I asked the owners if, instead of destroying it, I could have the martin house. They agreed, and after the old black locust pole was cut down, I took the pieces of the martin house home to rebuild. It took quite a few weekends to put the old martin house back into usable shape, but I'm proud to say that, after more than 100 years, that martin house is still serving as a home to these endearing birds.

This is the most complex of all the birdhouses in this book, and if you own a table saw, this is the project where it will really come in handy. Though some of the pieces can be cut from dimensional lumber, there is a fair amount of ripping involved to cut everything to size. And though you can do this with a circular saw and an edge guide, it will go a lot faster with a table saw.

This martin house design is based on that same martin house I scavenged all those years ago, with a few updates. It's built from clear pine, and has entrance holes that are situated 2" above the floor of each box (some recent research indicates that this height helps keep nestlings from inadvertently tumbling out of their compartments). It's designed to last many years, but be forewarned: this box is very heavy. Make sure you have help when it comes time to raise it into the air!

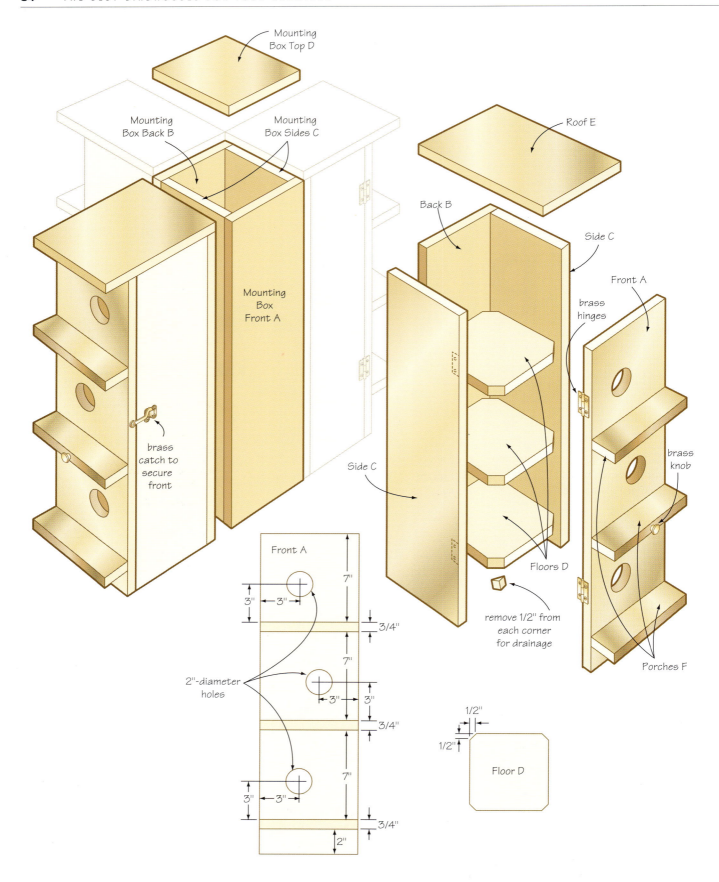

Mounting Box Top D

Mounting Box Back B

Mounting Box Sides C

Mounting Box Front A

brass catch to secure front

Roof E

Back B

Side C

brass hinges

Front A

Side C

Floors D

brass knob

remove 1/2" from each corner for drainage

Porches F

Front A

7"

3"   3"

3/4"

7"

2"-diameter holes

3"   3"

3/4"

7"

3"   3"

3/4"

2"

1/2"

1/2"

Floor D

Schedule of Materials: **PURPLE MARTIN HOUSE**

LETTER	QUANTITY	PART	STOCK	THICKNESS	WIDTH	LENGTH	COMMENTS
Apartments							
A	4	Fronts	1×8	$3/4$	$7^{1}/_{2}$	$25^{1}/_{4}$	
B	4	Backs	1×8	$3/4$	$7^{1}/_{2}$	$25^{1}/_{4}$	
C	8	Sides	1×8	$3/4$	6	$25^{1}/_{4}$	Rip to width from 1×8 stock.
D	12	Floors	1×8	$3/4$	6	6	Rip to width from 1×8 stock.
E	4	Roofs	1×8	$3/4$	$7^{1}/_{2}$	$10^{1}/_{2}$	
F	12	Porches	1×8	$3/4$	$7^{1}/_{2}$	$2^{3}/_{4}$	
Mounting Box							
A	1	Front	1×8	$3/4$	$7^{1}/_{2}$	$25^{1}/_{4}$	
B	1	Back	1×8	$3/4$	$7^{1}/_{2}$	$25^{1}/_{4}$	
C	2	Sides	1×8	$3/4$	6	$25^{1}/_{4}$	Rip to width from 1×8 stock.
D	1	Top	1×8	$3/4$	$7^{1}/_{2}$	$7^{1}/_{2}$	

Hardware and Supplies
- $1^{5}/_{8}$" galvanized screws
- 8 small brass hinges
- 4 brass latch sets
- 4 brass knobs
- Waterproof glue

About the Purple Martin

Whole books have been written about purple martins and how to attract them to your yard. There are also literally hundreds of groups across the country dedicated to purple martin conservation, and their members are so dedicated to the task that estimates indicate they spend more than $30 million each year on their endeavors. So rather than go into depth about this species, I'll just touch on its highlights. To learn more, check out the references listed in the back of this book. There you'll find listings for some of the major purple martin conservation groups in the United States.

Purple martins are the largest of the swallows in North America. Considered by many to be the first "true" bird of spring, they are a migratory species that returns each year from their Brazilian wintering grounds. Males usually arrive first and set out their territories, and females arrive a few days later.

Purple martins usually nest in colonies that number anywhere from just a few pairs up to as many as a hundred. They are very social, and will use groups of individual boxes, large apartments (as is this project) and clusters of hanging gourds. But remember that only about 10 percent of all purple martin houses actually have purple martins nesting in them. This species faces tremendous competition from European starlings and house sparrows, both introduced species that wreck havoc on all cavity-nesting native species.

House Placement

The purple martin house needs to be out in the open near water. The house should be anywhere from 12 to 20 feet in the air, and at least 30 feet away from any other structures (the further away, the better). Because of the necessity of frequent cleaning, monitoring and sparrow-evicting, the purple martin house also should be mounted on some form of pole system that is easy to raise or lower. Otherwise, you'll have to drag out an extension ladder every time you need access to it. Also, if possible, take down your martin house every fall. That way you'll ensure that it remains free of uninvited guests, and you'll have a chance to do maintenance on it during the winter months.

vital statistics

Purple Martin
(Progne subis)

SIZE:
$7^{1}/_{4}$" to $8^{1}/_{2}$"

NUMBER OF EGGS:
Usually 4 or 5

LENGTH OF INCUBATION:
15 to 18 days

BROODS PER SEASON:
Usually 1

FOOD:
All forms of flying insects

RANGE:
Summer only, East Coast west to the Rockies, and isolated colonies throughout the Pacific Coast

tip

To keep down the interior temperature of the purple martin house, give the outside surfaces a few coats of white exterior latex house paint. The white paint deflects the sun.

1

MEASURE FOR LENGTH

Based on the Schedule of Materials and illustration, make your measurements for the lengths of the backs, fronts, sides, roofs, floors and porches. Remember to allow for the kerf of the saw blade.

3 **ALLOW FOR DRAINAGE**

Cut away 1/2" from each corner of every floor to allow for proper drainage. Here I've simply set the miter gauge on the table saw to 45°, but you could use a jigsaw to do this just as easily.

2 **RIP TO WIDTH**

After crosscutting the boards to length, set your rip fence to the appropriate mark and rip the pieces to width where necessary. Remember to feed the work pieces through the saw with push sticks during this operation and to always keep your hands away from spinning blades. If you don't have a table saw, you can achieve the same results by clamping down an edge guide (such as a metal rule) and cutting along it with a circular saw.

ATTACH THE LEFT SIDE

Using the same procedure, attach the left side to the back of the first tower assembly.

4 | **BEGIN THE ASSEMBLY FOR THE FIRST TOWER**

To build this martin house, we're going to work in sections, with each of the four tower-shaped sides being an individual section. So to start the assembly on the first of the four towers, use 1⅝" screws and waterproof glue to attach the right-hand side to the back.

6 | **ADD THE FLOORS**

Add the floors for each of the three compartments in this tower. First, using screws, attach the floor for the top-most nesting compartment 7" below the top edge of the back piece. Next, attach the floor for the middle nesting compartment 7" below the bottom of the topmost floor. And finally, attach the floor for the bottom nesting compartment 7" below the bottom of the middle nesting compartment floor. Make sure that each floor is level front to back, and side to side.

8

DOUBLE-CHECK

Once you have the three floors and the roof attached, you should have a nesting tower that looks like this. Take a moment to double-check that everything is level and that all the joints are tight and secure. Purple martins are very susceptible to damp environments, and will quickly leave a nesting site if it fails to be weatherproof.

7 | **ATTACH THE ROOF**

With 1⅝" screws and waterproof glue, attach the roof to the top of the first tower.

9

BUILD THREE MORE TOWERS

Repeat Steps 4 through 8 to build another three more nesting towers. When you're finished, you'll have four complete towers that should look like the ones shown here.

purple martin house

10

MARK THE ENTRANCES

On the front piece for each of the four towers, draw lines that correspond with the tops of each of the three floors. For the top nesting compartment, make a mark that is 3" up from the floor line you just drew, and 3" from the left-hand edge of the front piece. Make a second mark for the middle nesting compartment that is 3" up from its floor line and 3" in from the right-hand edge of the front piece. For the bottom nesting compartment, make a mark that is 3" up from the bottom floor line, and 3" in from the left-hand edge of the front.

11 CUT THE ENTRANCES

With your 2" hole saw, drill out the entrance holes on all four front pieces that you just marked. Remember that there is a specific orientation to the holes; the top entrance hole is closest to the left-hand edge of the front piece for each of the four units.

12 ATTACH THE PORCHES

Using 1⅝" screws and waterproof glue, attach the porches to each of the four front pieces. Make sure that the top of the porches aligns with the floor lines you drew in Step 10. Once you have all three porches attached, the front pieces should look like the one shown here.

13 | ATTACH THE HINGES

Attach the hinges to the front and to the tower assembly. Make sure that the hinges are straight, so that the front can be opened easily and that there are no gaps.

14 | ONE COMPLETED TOWER

This is how one completed tower should look, before you've attached the latches.

15 | ATTACH THE LATCHES

Center a brass latch on the middle nesting compartment of each tower, and attach it to both the door and the side. Make sure it fits snugly so that there is no chance of the wind opening it or a predator lifting it and gaining access to the nests inside.

16

ATTACH THE KNOBS

Screw a brass knob onto the face of the middle porch of each tower. These aren't really necessary, but I like the elegant look they lend the structure.

17 | **BEGIN THE MOUNTING BOX**

With 1⁵⁄₈" screws and waterproof glue, attach one of the sides to the back of the center mounting box.

18 | **ATTACH THE OPPOSITE SIDE**

With the same technique, attach the other side of the center mounting box to the back.

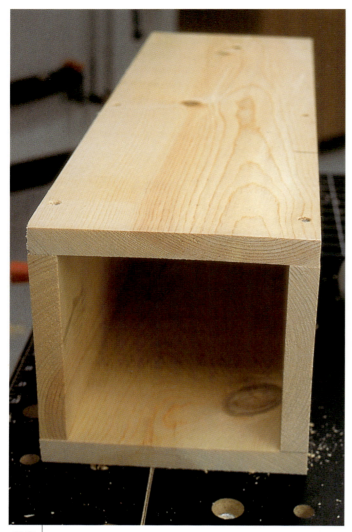

20 | ATTACH THE TOWERS TO THE CENTER MOUNTING BOX

Align one of the nesting towers with one of the sides of the center mounting box, and through the back of the tower, drill the mounting holes for 1⁵⁄₈" screws into the center mounting box. Repeat the process for all remaining towers until you have built a cross-like structure.

19 | ATTACH THE FRONT

Again with glue and screws, attach the front to the center mounting box.

21 | ADD THE ROOF

Using glue and screws, attach the roof to the center mounting box.

22

ADD VENTILATION HOLES

Drill two ¹/₄" holes into each side of every nesting compartment to allow for proper ventilation.

23 | **SAND**

Sand the entire surface. I like to spend a little extra time sanding when I build a martin house, because I know I'll be handling it quite a bit through the years. Round over any corners and edges, and make a final check to ensure that everything is fitting together tightly.

things to look out for

Keep an eye out for predators such as cats, raccoons, snakes and other climbing animals.

House sparrows and European starlings love to steal space in purple martin houses. Consider not erecting your house until after these species have begun their nest-building activities. Don't be afraid of tearing out the nests of unwanted tenants.

Tree swallows also like to use purple martin houses. If you have a problem with them, block off the holes of the martin house until the tree swallows have established their nests elsewhere.

It is not easy to get a colony of purple martins established. Be prepared to invest considerable amounts of time in the effort — it will be well worth it.

butterfly
house

Here's a project that's sure to brighten up not just your garden, but your day as well. After all, who can help but feel cheerful when they see butterflies flitting about? And this butterfly home will ensure that the garden visitors of the summer survive the cold of winter. This project is quite simple. It is built from Douglas fir, though any rot-resistant wood would be a good choice.

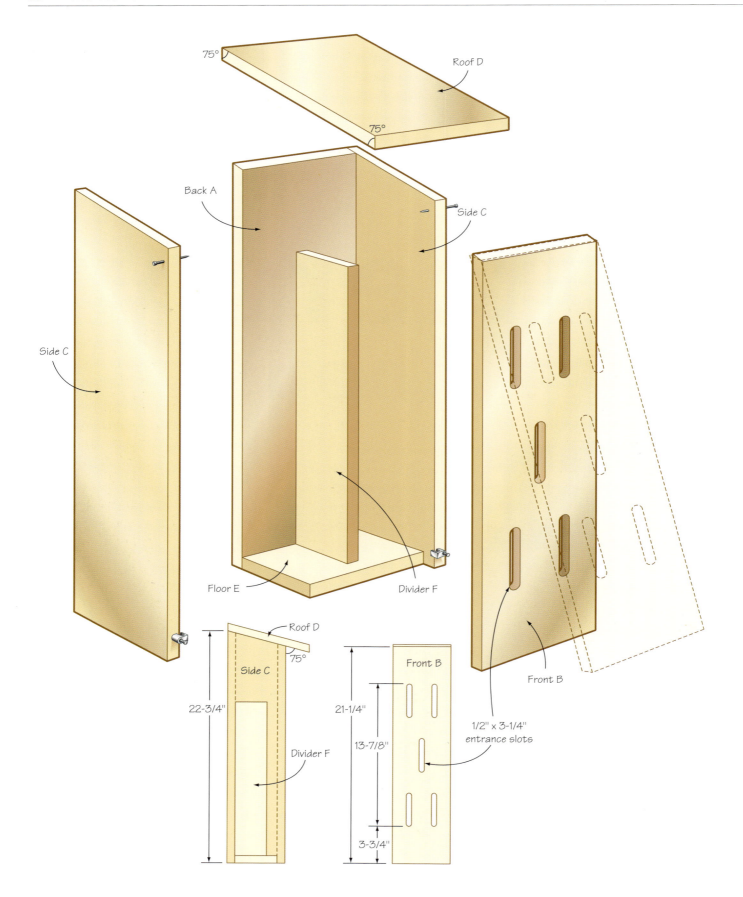

75°

Roof D

75°

Back A

Side C

Side C

Floor E

Divider F

Side C

Front B

Front B

1/2" x 3-1/4" entrance slots

Roof D

75°

Side C

Divider F

22-3/4"

Front B

21-1/4"

13-7/8"

3-3/4"

butterfly house

Schedule of Materials: **BUTTERFLY HOUSE**

LETTER	QUANTITY	PART	STOCK	THICKNESS	WIDTH	LENGTH	COMMENTS
A	1	Back	1×6	3/4	5 1/2	22 3/4	
B	1	Front	1×6	3/4	5 1/2	21 1/4	Cut five 1/2" x 3 1/4" entrance slots.
C	2	Sides	1×6	3/4	5 1/2	22 3/4	Tapers to 21 1/4" at front edge.
D	1	Roof	1×8	3/4	6 1/2	7 3/4	
E	1	Floor	1×6	3/4	4	5 1/2	
F	1	Divider	1×6	3/4	3	15	

Hardware and Supplies

• 1 5/8" galvanized screws

• Waterproof glue

• Audiovisual cable stays

• 1 1/2" galvanized finishing nails

Why Butterflies Need Homes

Butterflies are a delight to behold. Their bright, cheerful colors and happy, carefree, flight never fail to amuse both young and old. And butterflies play a crucial role in the development of our flower gardens since they aid in pollination. But did you know that some of these delicate creatures actually hibernate in the winter? Though most species fly south to warmer weather, some species prefer to stick it out, hiding themselves away in nooks and crannies such as behind the bark of trees and in woodpiles. Some of the species that hibernate are:

• Comma anglewings
• Mourning cloaks
• Red admirals
• Painted ladies
• Queens
• Question marks

Butterfly houses also serve double-duty. During the summer months, they can serve as a shelter from bad weather, as well as a hiding place for just about any butterfly species trying to evade a predator.

House Placement

Mount your butterfly house on a pole or post about 3 to 4 feet in the air. It needs two different placements: one for summer and one for winter. During the summer months, a location in and around tall flowering plants is the best. Once winter sets in, move the house to a sheltered place out of the wind and protected from moisture.

Plants that Attract Butterflies

If you're just trying to attract butterflies to your garden, consider adding some of the following plants around your yard. Some of these even grow wild, so think twice when you're weeding — you may already have a plant that's ideal for butterflies.

• Alfalfa
• Aster
• Black-Eyed Susan
• Butterfly Bush
• Daisies
• Dogbane
• Goldenrod
• Lantana
• Lupine
• Marigolds
• Mint
• Privet
• Purple coneflower
• Queen Anne's Lace
• Red clover
• Sweet pea
• Winter Cress

working with douglas fir

Douglas fir is a good wood for birdhouse projects. It's weather-resistant but doesn't have the price tag that comes with cedar or cypress. But Douglas fir can be tricky to work with. At times, it may seem as if the wood has a mind of its own, especially when you're trying to drill holes. You'll be all lined up, start to drill, and the next thing you know, your drill is skewing sideways. This behavior is common with Douglas fir. To prevent this from happening, always make sure the wood is clamped down securely, and work slowly. For drilling, if you have access to a drill press, use it — you'll be much happier with the results.

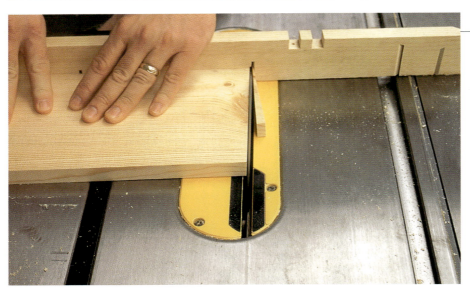

1

MEASURE AND CUT

Based on the dimensions in the Schedule of Materials and on the illustration, take all measurements and cut the pieces to size. For the sides, the miter gauge of a table saw is handy.

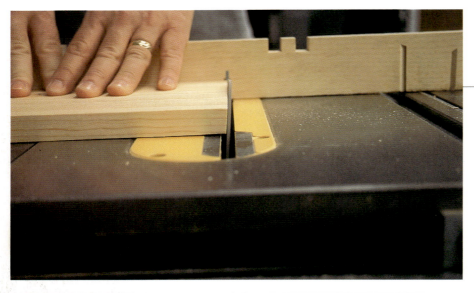

2

BEVEL THE FRONT AND BACK

Since the roof sits at a slope, bevel the top edges of both the front and back pieces. Take the angle you'll need from one of the sides with a bevel gauge (see "Other Hand Tools" on page 14), and then set the table saw or circular saw angle based on that measurement.

3

ATTACH THE FLOOR

Using 1⁵⁄₈" galvanized screws or 1¹⁄₂" galvanized nails and waterproof glue, attach the floor to the back.

butterfly house

4

ATTACH THE DIVIDER

Mount the internal divider to the back and floor using waterproof glue and 1⁵⁄₈" screws or 1¹⁄₂" galvanized nails.

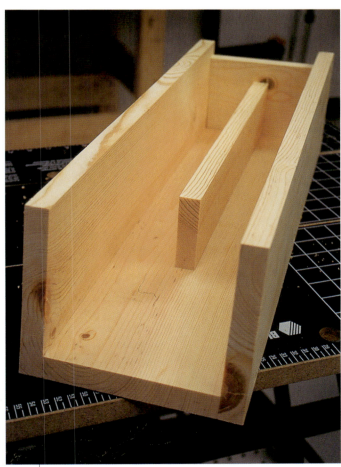

6 **MARK THE ENTRANCE HOLES**

Measure and mark the location for the five ¹⁄₂" × 3¹⁄₄" entrance holes on the front.

5 **ATTACH THE SIDES**

Clamp the sides to the back and floor and, with waterproof glue and 1⁵⁄₈" screws, attach them to the house assembly.

8

CUT OUT THE ENTRANCES

With a jigsaw or coping saw, cut from one hole to another to complete the entrance holes.

7 | **DRILL TERMINAL POINTS**
With a $1/2$" bit, drill the terminal points for each of the five entrance holes as shown here.

9

ATTACH THE FRONT

Clamp the front piece in place. Secure it to the house assembly with two $1\frac{1}{2}$" finishing nails driven through the side pieces. (The nails will serve as pivoting points.) Use audiovisual cable stays to serve as locks for the front.

butterfly house

10 DOUBLE-CHECK

This is how the box should look so far, and how the pivoting front should function. This is a good time to check for fit and movement to make sure that nothing is binding and that all the joints are watertight and weatherproof.

11 ATTACH THE ROOF

Mount the roof to the butterfly house assembly. I wanted to keep the screw heads to a minimum, so I used polyurethane glue. Do not apply any glue to the front edge, as that front piece will need to be free to pivot open for cleaning.

12 SAND

Once the glue has cured, sand everything down, and the project is completed.

bat
house

As a member of the National Speleological Society, and an avid caver, I have a special fondness for bats. I had often seen them flitting about at twilight, but it wasn't until I started caving that I got "up close and personal" with these little creatures. Now, rather than having to wait outside to catch a glimpse of them in their nightly feeding flights, I can crawl right into their living room and see what they're up to!

You, too, can get up close and personal with bats by building a bat house. The one you see here is a perfect little starter home. It is designed for one of the most common bat species, the little brown bat. It's constructed from cedar and is quite simple to build. It's another one of those projects that's perfect for young hands. And after all, what child wouldn't get a kick out of telling their friends that they built a bat house instead of a birdhouse.

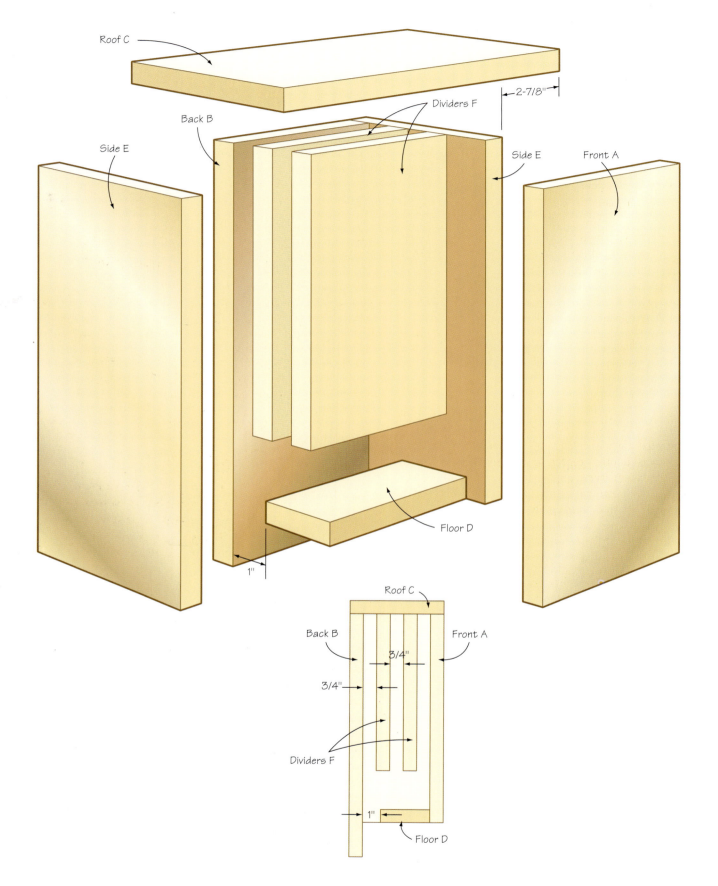

Roof C

Dividers F

2-7/8"

Back B

Side E

Side E

Front A

Floor D

1"

Roof C

Back B

Front A

3/4"

3/4"

Dividers F

1"

Floor D

Schedule of Materials: **BAT HOUSE**

LETTER	QUANTITY	PART	STOCK	THICKNESS	WIDTH	LENGTH	COMMENTS
A	1	Front	1×6	3/4	5 1/4	12	
B	1	Back	1×6	3/4	5 1/4	14	
C	1	Roof	1×6	3/4	5 1/4	11	
D	1	Floor	1×6	3/4	5 1/4	2 3/4	
E	2	Sides	1×6	3/4	5 1/4	12	
F	2	Dividers	1×6	3/4	5 1/4	9	

Hardware and Supplies
- 1 5/8" galvanized screws
- Polyurethane glue

About the Little Brown Bat

The little brown bat is the most common bat throughout the middle to northern parts of the United States and in Canada. It is a small creature, only about 3½" in length, with a wingspan of about 8". Its name is somewhat misleading, as the little brown bat can vary in color from yellowish to nearly all black.

The little brown bat is an insectivore. On average, one little brown bat can eat as many as 500 insects in just one hour. Think what a whole colony could do in a night! Just another reason to want to attract these creatures to your property.

The little brown bat is unique in its reproductive habits. Mating starts in late August and continues into the winter. Sperm is stored in the uterus, and ovulation and fertilization are delayed until spring when the female emerges from hibernation. Young (usually just one) are born in June and July after a gestation period of 50 to 60 days. The young begin to fly at 18 days of age. After 3 weeks they have reached their adult size.

Bats are relatively quiet creatures. The high-intensity FM echolocation used by the little brown bat is difficult for the human ear to detect. "Clicks" can sometimes be heard as the bats are hunting and diving for food and especially when they are distressed.

Hearing Ranges

Since the little brown bat uses echolocation to find its food in the dark, it has evolved very sensitive hearing. Take a look at its hearing range, and compare it to other animals.

ANIMAL	FREQUENCY (HERTZ)	
	LOW	HIGH
Bats	1,000	150,000
Humans	20	20,000
Cats	100	32,000
Dogs	40	46,000
Horses	31	40,000
Elephants	16	12,000
Cattle	16	40,000
Grasshoppers and locusts	100	50,000
Rodents	1,000	100,000
Whales and dolphins	70	150,000
Seals and sea lions	200	55,000

House Placement

One of the most important factors in house placement for bats is temperature. Bats are extremely sensitive to heat and cold. The little brown bat needs at least four hours of sun a day. Some folks have also painted their houses black or covered them in tar paper to help them better absorb sunlight energy.

Height is also important in house placement. Bats like houses that are high up — the higher, the better. One of the reasons for this is the way bats take flight. Bats don't just wing away like a bird. Before they can fly, they need to drop through some vertical space beneath them; only then will they flap their wings and be able to take to the skies.

One last factor to consider when placing your bat house is insect populations. If you can place the house within a quarter mile of water, you'll stand a better chance of attracting occupants. Because of the bats' tremendous appetite for insects, such as mosquitoes, any place that has ideal conditions for insect populations will be a good place for a bat house.

vital statistics

Little Brown Bat
(Myotis lucifugus)

SIZE:
3½" long

FOOD:
Insects of all sorts, but especially mosquitoes

RANGE:
Continental United States, north to Canada

tip

When building this project, make sure the rough side of the cedar always faces in. That way, the bats will have a better gripping surface from which to cling as they roost.

painting bat houses

Bats need warm environments, especially during winter when they hibernate. If you live in a northern area, know that little brown bats, in general, need at least 4 hours of sun and warmth each day in order to survive. Painting your bat house black can increase the warming potential of the house. Bats in southern climates, especially in the American Southwest, need cooler areas. Because of this need, consider leaving the bat house unpainted. Remember the amount of warmth can vary from species to species: For example, big brown bats need 7 hours of sun in the winter, compared to 4 hours needed by the little brown bat. Determine the type of bat you're most likely to attract and make your painting decisions accordingly.

1

MEASURE
Based on the Schedule of Materials and illustration, measure out the pieces for the bat house. Remember to allow for the kerf of the saw blade.

2

CUT TO SIZE
Based on the measurements you just took, cut the pieces to size.

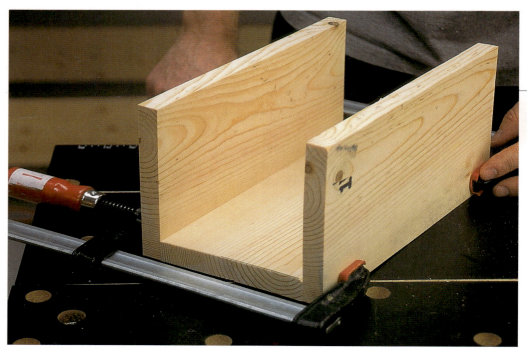

3

GLUE ON THE SIDES
Using polyurethane glue, attach the sides to the back. Use clamps to hold the pieces in place until the glue cures.

bat house

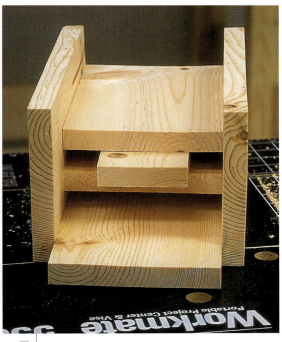

4 | **ADD IN THE FIRST DIVIDER**

With polyurethane glue, attach the first divider to the sides. Use some ³/₄" thick scrap material as a spacer to ensure the correct gap between the back piece and the divider.

5 | **ADD IN THE SECOND DIVIDER**

Using the same technique as in Step 4, attach the second divider.

6 | **ADD THE FRONT**

Again with polyurethane glue, add the front piece and clamp until the glue cures.

things to look out for

The accumulation of urine and feces in an established bat house can be a cause for concern. A fungus that finds ideal growing conditions in this built-up fecal matter can cause a lung disease called histoplasmosis. In general, the amount of fecal matter will not build up in a small bat house where it would present any severe health threats. However, as a general precaution, always wear rubber gloves and a nose-and-mouth filter mask. Another concern is the incidence of rabies in bats; however, it is much lower than in other native mammals, as the little brown bat is not capable of biting and breaking human skin. Nevertheless, never pick up an injured bat, or handle them in any way. Bats do not like drafts of any sort. Make sure your bat house fits together very snugly and is completely weatherproof.

no pivoting bottom

Many bat houses incorporate a pivoting bottom to allow for clean-out. My design does not allow for this for a number of reasons. First, I don't like to disturb bats in any way. They seem to be finicky and a bit temperamental when it comes to their housing sites, so I upset them as little as possible once they are established. Second, the design of this house is so small that the buildup of feces and urine deposits would not present a significant health problem. If you would like to add a pivoting option, however, it would be simple enough to use finishing nails as pivots for the bottom, instead of gluing it into place. You could then use wood screws to secure it in place, as audiovisual cable stays would not necessarily be strong enough to endure the bats' comings and goings.

7

ADD THE ROOF

Glue on the roof as you did the front piece.

8

ADD THE FLOOR

Glue in the floor and clamp until the glue has cured. Though many designs call for a pivoting panel on the bottom to facilitate clean-out, I prefer a glued-in piece to ensure weather protection and to minimize drafts.

9

SAND

Smooth out the outer faces of the roosting box, and it's ready for use!

bat house

the strangest bat house ever built

Though the bat house project here is a small one, some people have taken the task of attracting bats to extreme measures. Take for example the case of Mr. Richter Clyde Perky. At one time, Mr. Perky probably controlled more land in the Florida Keys than any other person. One of his holdings was a parcel of land on Sugarloaf Key, where he dreamed of opening a vacation and fishing resort. But in order for his dreams to come to fruition, he knew he would have to find a way to deal with the voracious Florida mosquitoes. He had seen large bat homes used successfully in Texas, and he thought a bat house was the ideal answer to the mosquito problem. So in 1929 he built his resort and constructed a massive bat tower of Dade County pine. Thirty feet tall, it towered above the mangrove trees. But after its construction, no local bats took up residence.

Perky was not one to give up easily. Since bats weren't coming voluntarily, he imported them — only to have every single one take off and never return to roost. Still not daunted, he made up a mixture of bat guano and ground-up female bat sex organs to "seed" the tower and attract bats. But, still, no bats took up permanent residence.

Well, as nature would have it, a hurricane wiped out the fishing resort, Perky finally gave up and the mangroves reclaimed most of the property. But the tower still stands. No other sign of Perky's resort can be found, and unfortunately, neither can any bats, even to this day!

BILL KEOGH © 2000

sunflower
seed
feeder

Feeding birds has been part of my life for so long, that I can't remember a time when I wasn't involved with the activity. My great aunts and my father have all been avid devotees of bird feeding, too. It's always a delight to see how many different types of birds I can lure to my backyard in the winter. Plus, a bird's bright plumage adds such cheery color to an expanse of blank, white snow.

I've put two feeder plans in this book — this one for a simple sunflower seed feeder and one for a suet feeder (see Project 13). This sunflower seed feeder is a modified version of one the Cub Scouts build in the pack where I'm Assistant Cubmaster. It's an easy project, and its open design will attract many different species of birds. But keep an eye out for squirrels, as the design also allows easy access for these voracious eaters as well!

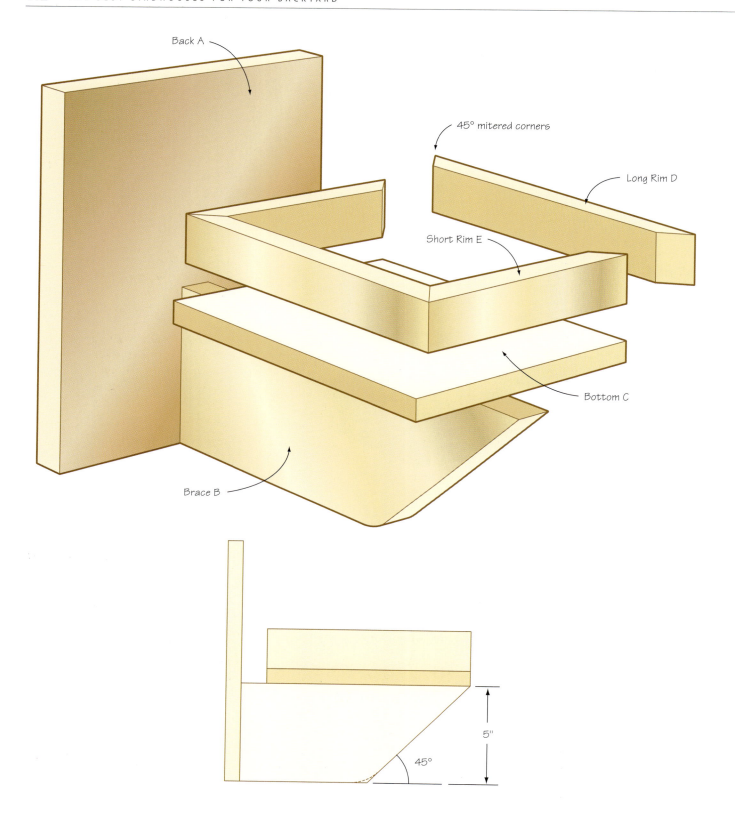

Back A

45° mitered corners

Long Rim D

Short Rim E

Bottom C

Brace B

5"

45°

Schedule of Materials: SUNFLOWER SEED FEEDER

LETTER	QUANTITY	PART	STOCK	THICKNESS	WIDTH	LENGTH	COMMENTS
A	1	Back	1×10	$\frac{3}{4}$	$9\frac{1}{4}$	$12\frac{1}{4}$	
B	1	Brace	1×12	$\frac{3}{4}$	5	$11\frac{1}{4}$	
C	1	Bottom	1×10	$\frac{3}{4}$	$7\frac{3}{4}$	10	Rip to width.
D	2	Long Rims	1×2	1	2	10	
E	2	Short Rims	1×2	1	2	$7\frac{3}{4}$	

Hardware and Supplies

• $1\frac{5}{8}$" galvanized screws

• Waterproof glue

About Feeding Birds

Feeding birds provides entertainment and enjoyment for people of all ages. You can attract birds to your backyard throughout the year, but the most important time to help the birds is during the winter. Then, cold temperatures and snow limit the food supply and put extra demands on birds to keep warm, unlike during the warmer months, when birds feed on insects.

Once you begin feeding during the winter, don't stop. Birds become dependent on a food source and may not locate an alternative once you stop feeding them. There are a variety of seeds and foods that attract birds. The development of black oil sunflower seeds revolutionized bird feeding. It is the single favorite and most nutritious food for birds. Adding specialty foods to feeders will attract even a wider variety of birds. In the summer, for example, sugar water attracts hummingbirds; fruit brings northern orioles, waxwings, blue jays and thrashers; and mealworms can lure bluebirds. In the spring and fall, thistle seed will attract the Harris' sparrow and red-breasted nuthatch. A mixture of black oil sunflower and thistle seeds attracts evening grosbeaks, redpolls and pine siskins during the winter. Niger thistle attracts purplefinches, housefinches and goldfinches all year long. Suet will be utilized regularly by woodpeckers, nuthatches and chickadees.

Feeder Placement

Placement of your feeder is as important as the feed you put in it. First, consider where you want to watch your birds. Is it by a window, a glass door, or from the second story? Pick a feeder location that is easily accessible for filling with food and one that's out of the wind. Also consider the mess that empty and spilled seeds will cause below the feeder. Finally, it's important to keep unwanted predators, such as stray cats, away from your feeder. Cats kill millions of songbirds annually and should be prevented from climbing near feeders.

things to look out for

Check your feeder for cleanliness — a dirty feeder may cause disease or discourage birds from coming.

If you have trouble attracting birds, try adding a water source.

Local bird populations will fluctuate, however, and birds absent for a period of time should not concern you.

1

MEASURE
Based on the Schedule of Materials and illustration, measure out the pieces for the feeder. Remember to allow for the kerf of the saw blade.

2

CUT TO SIZE

Based on the measurements you just took, cut the pieces to size.

3

CUT THE BRACE

When cutting the brace, it's easiest to first cut a rectangular shape and then cut it to its final dimensions.

CUT THE LONG AND SHORT RIMS

Cut out the long and short rims to their rough length from stock 1×2 material.

MITER THE LONG AND SHORT RIMS

Miter the ends of the long and short rims at 45° so that you'll be able to frame in the bottom. A table saw or miter saw works great for this job.

ATTACH LONG RIMS

Glue the long rims onto the bottom and clamp until dry.

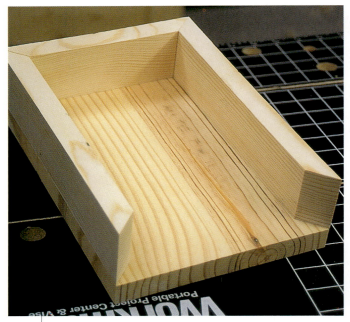

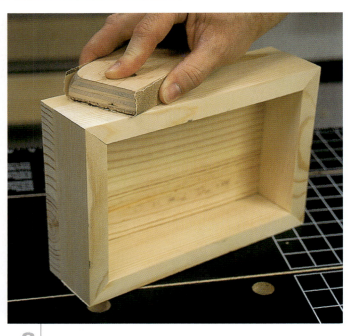

7 | **ATTACH ONE SHORT RIM**
Now glue in place just one of the short rims and clamp until dry.

8 | **ATTACH THE FINAL SHORT RIM AND SAND**
Lastly, glue in place the remaining short rim. I assemble the rims in this fashion as final adjustments to the last rim are often needed due to wood warp or other defects. If all of the other three rims are secure, it narrows the variables, and any adjustments then have to be made to only one piece. Before attaching the tray to the brace, take a moment and sand everything down.

9

ATTACH THE TRAY TO THE BASE
Use three $1\frac{5}{8}$" galvanized screws to attach the tray to the base.

sunflower seed feeder

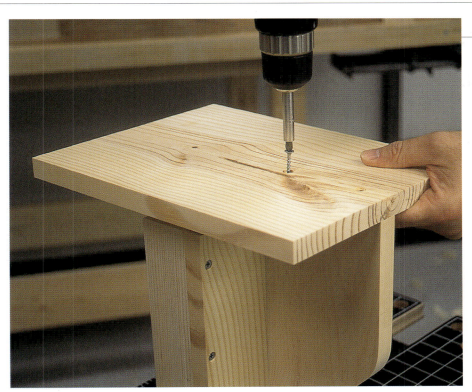

10
ATTACH THE BACK

With two $1\frac{5}{8}$" screws, attach the back to the brace. Make sure the bottom of the brace aligns flush with the bottom edge of the back.

11
FINISH SANDING

Now that everything is complete, give the feeder one last sanding.

suet
feeder

While sunflower seeds do a great job of attracting and providing for songbirds, what about the local woodpeckers? They too go through a great deal of hardship in the winter. Well, here's the perfect project for them — a suet feeder. Suet, a blend of hard animal fats, makes a great winter food for woodpeckers, flickers and nuthatches. Made with Douglas fir, this suet feeder is a snap to build and maintain, and its size makes it ideal for even the smallest settings.

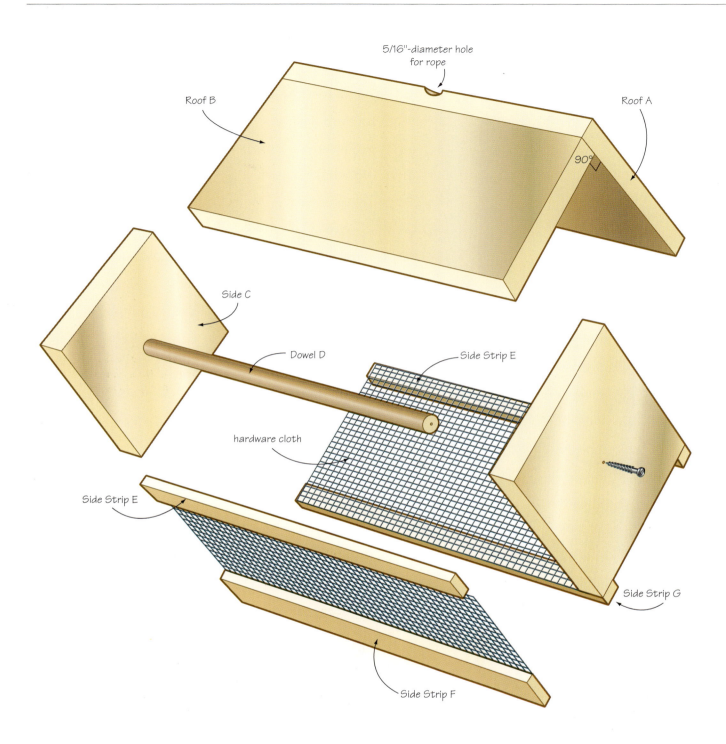

5/16"-diameter hole for rope

Roof B

Roof A

90°

Side C

Dowel D

Side Strip E

hardware cloth

Side Strip E

Side Strip G

Side Strip F

suet feeder

Schedule of Materials: SUET FEEDER

LETTER	QUANTITY	PART	STOCK	THICKNESS	WIDTH	LENGTH	COMMENTS
A	1	Roof	1×6	$3/4$	$5^{1}/_{2}$	10	
B	1	Roof	1×6	$3/4$	$4^{3}/_{4}$	10	Rip to width.
C	2	Sides	1×6	$3/4$	$4^{3}/_{4}$	$4^{3}/_{4}$	
D	1	Rod	Dowel	$1/2$ dia.		$9^{1}/_{4}$	
E	2	Strip	scrap	$1/4$	1	10	Rip to thickness and width.
F	1	Strip	scrap	$1/4$	1	10	Rip to thickness and width.
G	1	Strip	scrap	$1/4$	$3/4$	10	Rip to thickness and width.

Hardware and Supplies

- $1^{5}/_{8}$" galvanized screws
- $9^{1}/_{2}$" × 10" hardware cloth ($1/2$" × $1/2$" mesh) or other screening
- $1/4$" nylon rope (to hang feeder)
- Staples and staple gun
- Polyurethane glue

1

MEASURE

Based on the Schedule of Materials and illustration, make all your measurements for the parts of the suet feeder. Remember to allow for the kerf of the saw blade.

2

CUT THE ROOF TO LENGTH

Based on the measurements you just made, cut the roof pieces to their proper length.

3

RIP THE ROOF

Since one roof section needs to be slightly narrower than the other, rip one of the roof sections to the narrower width specified in the Schedule of Materials.

4 | **GLUE THE ROOF**

The two roof sections need to be butt-jointed together, so apply a liberal amount of polyurethane glue to the edge of the narrower piece, clamp it to the other roof section, and allow to dry.

5 | **CUT THE SIDES**

Based on the measurements you made in Step 1, cut the side panels to their correct length.

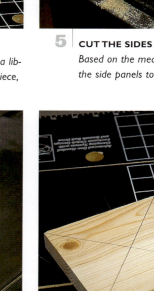

6 | **RIP THE SIDES**

Now rip the sides so that you have a square piece that measures $4^{3}/_{4}$" × $4^{3}/_{4}$".

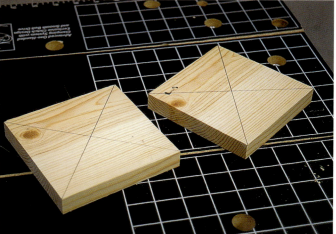

7 | **MARK THE CENTERS**

Draw pencil lines from corner to corner on each of the two sides to mark the center points. You'll need to know where the centers are so that you can accurately drill for the center rod.

8 | **DRILL THE CENTER HOLES**

Since you'll need to drill a ¹/₂"-diameter by ³/₈"-deep hole for the center rod, take some masking tape and wrap it around your ¹/₂" drill bit at the correct depth. That way, you'll be sure not to inadvertently drill through the sides.

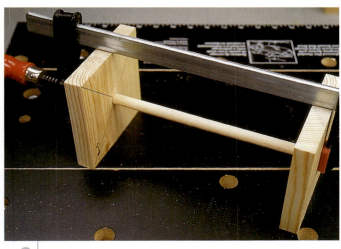

9 | **GLUE IN THE ROD**

With polyurethane glue and screws, attach the center rod in place and let dry. Make sure each of the sides are square with each other, by holding them in place with clamps.

10 | **DRILL FOR THE CORD**

Drill a hole through the roof at the center point to allow for the hanging cord.

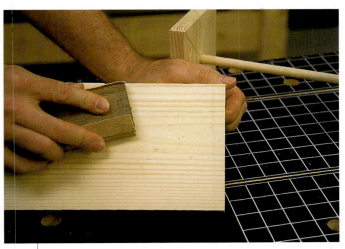

11 | **SAND AND FINAL ASSEMBLY**

Sand everything down to remove any imperfections. Then fold and staple a 9¹/₂" × 10" piece of ¹/₂" × ¹/₂" mesh hardware cloth to the bottom two edges of the sides as shown in the illustration. Lastly feed a ¹/₄" nylon cord through the hole in the roof, tie to the center of the rod, fill with suet and your feeder is completed.

Entrance Hole Chart
(sizes shown to scale)

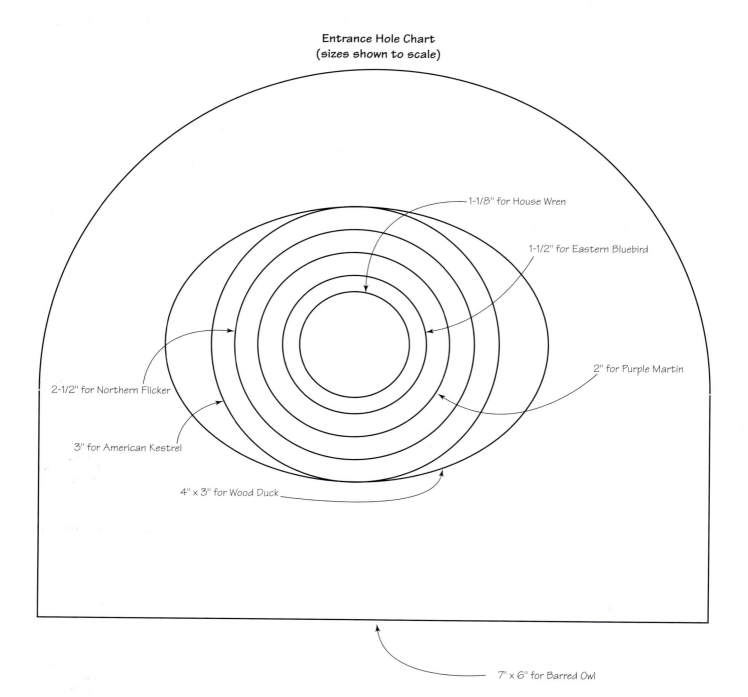

1-1/8" for House Wren

1-1/2" for Eastern Bluebird

2" for Purple Martin

2-1/2" for Northern Flicker

3" for American Kestrel

4" x 3" for Wood Duck

7" x 6" for Barred Owl

Common Adhesives

ADHESIVE	ADVANTAGES	DISADVANTAGES	COMMON USES	WORKING TIME	CLAMPING TIME (at 70° F)	CURE TIME	SOLVENT
Yellow glue (aliphatic resin)	Easy to use; water resistant; water cleanup; economical.	Not waterproof (don't use on outdoor furniture).	All-purpose wood glue for interior use; stronger bond than white glue.	5 to 7 minutes	1 to 2 hours	24 hours	Warm water
Contact cement	Bonds parts immediately.	Can't readjust parts after contact.	Bonding wood veneer or plastic laminate to substrate.	Up to 1 hour	No clamps; parts bond on contact	–	Acetone
Super glue (Cyanoacrylate)	Bonds parts quickly.	Limited to small parts.	Bonding small parts made from a variety of materials.	30 seconds	10 to 60 seconds; clamps usually not required	30 minutes to several hours	Acetone
Epoxy glue	Good gap filler; waterproof; fast setting formulas available; can be used to bond glass to metal or wood.	Requires mixing.	Bonding small parts made from a variety of materials.	5 to 60 minutes depending on epoxy formula	5 minutes to several hours depending on epoxy formula	3 hours and longer	Lacquer thinner
Animal glue, dry (hide glue)	Extended working time; water cleanup; economical.	Must be mixed with water and heated; poor moisture resistance (don't use on outdoor furniture).	Time-consuming assembly work; stronger bond than liquid animal glue; interior use only.	30 minutes	2 to 3 hours	24 hours	Warm water
Animal glue, liquid (hide glue)	Easy to use; extended working time; water cleanup; economical.	Poor moisture resistance (don't use on outdoor furniture).	Time-consuming assembly work; interior use only.	5 minutes	2 hours	24 hours	Warm water
Polyurethane	Fully waterproof; gap-filling.	Eye and skin irritant.	Multi-purpose, interior and exterior applications including wood to wood, ceramic, plastic, Corian, stone, metal.	30 minutes	1 to 2 hours	8 hours	Mineral spirits while wet; must abrade or scrape off when dry
White glue (polyvinyl acetate)	Easy to use; economical.	Not waterproof (don't use on outdoor furniture).	All-purpose wood glue for interior use; yellow glue has stronger bond.	3 to 5 minutes	16 hours	24 to 48 hours	Warm water and soap
Waterproof glue (resorcinol)	Fully waterproof; extended working time.	Requires mixing; dark color shows glue line on most woods; long clamping time.	Outdoor furniture, marine applications.	20 minutes	1 hour	12 hours	Cool water before hardening
Plastic resin (urea formaldehyde)	Good water resistance; economical.	Requires mixing; long clamping time.	Outdoor furniture, cutting boards.	15 to 30 minutes	6 hours	24 hours	Warm water and soap before hardening

resources

AMERICAN BIRDING ASSOCIATION
P.O. Box 6599
Colorado Springs, CO 80934
800-850-2473
www.americanbirding.org

DUCKS UNLIMITED, INC.
One Waterfowl Way
Memphis, TN 38120
800-45-DUCKS
www.ducks.org

DUCKS UNLIMITED CANADA
P.O. Box 1160
Stonewall, Manitoba ROC 2Z0
800-665-DUCK
www.ducks.ca/home.html

NATIONAL AUDUBON SOCIETY
700 Broadway
New York, NY 10003
212-979-3000
www.audubon.org

NATIONAL SPELEOLOGICAL SOCIETY
2813 Cave Avenue
Huntsville, AL 35810-4413
256-852-1300
www.caves.org

BAT CONSERVATION INTERNATIONAL
P.O. Box 162603
Austin, TX 78716
1-800-538-BATS
www.batcon.org

NORTH AMERICAN BLUEBIRD SOCIETY
Department L
P.O. Box 74
Darlington, WI 53530-0074
608-329-6403
www.nabluebirdsociety.org

PURPLE MARTIN CONSERVATION ASSOCIATION
Edinboro University
Edinboro, PA 16444
814-734-4420
www.purplemartin.org

THE PURPLE MARTIN SOCIETY, NA
8921 Royal Drive
Burr Ridge, IL 60521-8332
630-655-2028
www.purplemartins.com

index